The Art of Being Yourself

The Art of Being Yourself

~~~

FRANK E. RICHELIEU

*Discover Who You Are
and Learn How to Live*

Science of Mind Communications
Los Angeles, California

First Edition — August 1992

Cover design by Suzanne Kelley
Book design by Randall Friesen

Printed in the United States of America

Published by
SCIENCE OF MIND COMMUNICATIONS
3251 West Sixth Street, P.O. Box 75127, Los Angeles, CA 90075

Library of Congress Catalog Card Number: 92-053722

ISBN: 0-917849-15-9

*To my beloved wife, Anita, and my excep-
tional daughters, Laurie Grace, Holly Louise,
and Leslie Hope, whose involvement and
minor dilemmas added largely to the body of
this thirty years of work and my own personal
growth and unfolding in the art of being
yourself.*

Acknowledgments

Through the years, my enthusiastic supporters have voiced their "shoulds" to me: "You should write a book!" The idea escalated into a crescendo of "shoulds," tantamount to a guilt trip.

While many of my sincerest friends and supporters *know* exactly what I should do, the fact remains that my time is committed largely to the operations of our very large and rewarding center in Redondo Beach, and to the time-consuming media ministry in which I am involved.

To the following talented and loving individuals go my boundless thanks and credit for assisting in bringing forth the book:

>**My core of countless volunteers** who diligently transcribed hundreds of tape-recorded lessons and messages over a thirty-year span.

>**Reola Presley**, my first secretary and editor, who edited out the extraneous material, bringing my talks down to succinct, concise lessons.

>**Bill Stroup**, marketing professional, who was the catalyst that brought the project together.

>**Kathy Juline**, director of *Science of Mind* Communications, who believed in my work and unstintingly labored through the boxes and boxes of my material, organizing and sorting, and making sense of all my ramblings. In Ms. Juline, I have discovered a talent extraordinaire, and a mind brilliant enough to have written the book single-handedly.

>**Dr. Anita L. Richelieu**, my co-producer, ultimate editor, and valuable critic. To Dr. Anita go immeasurable praise and credit for the sharp pencil she applied to my undisciplined verbiage. In short, she makes me look good.

Contents

Preface

Throughout a span of nearly thirty-five years, my mission has been to lead people to self-leadership and dominion over all facts and conditions in their lives. Willpower alone doesn't seem to work, nor does success come about simply through chance or luck. In fact, I have observed that, in reality, we are the creators of our luck.

How and why we create our lives the way we do has been the central core of my study and research. When I was a student of Dr. Ernest Holmes, who founded the Science of Mind philosophy, the method to use in conducting my research became clear: begin with a premise and see if the data bears out that premise. My premise was: *Perfect Cause, or Creative Power; Perfect Man/Woman; Perfect Being.*

In order to prove the premise, *Perfect Cause, Perfect Man/Woman, Perfect Being,* I had to observe a perfect, initiating power moving through individual lives, yours and mine, to the ultimate end: a successful, fulfilling result. This is where the challenge began.

For some people, the perfect power seemed to glide through their lives, bringing a succession of blessings to warm the heart. For others, who appeared to be equally talented and deserving, nothing seemed to go well. They struggled and toiled day and night in diverse fields of expression. Their businesses withered, their personal lives failed, and their physical health suffered in the balance.

My premise expanded to include a catalyst—*freedom of choice.* Exercising this freedom, humanity can choose either to believe in its own innate perfection and divine empowerment or to think of itself as unworthy, undeserving, helpless and hopeless.

A pattern began to emerge. I started to find the connecting links between cause and effect. The mental causes which we were activating in our lives evolved out of our personal beliefs— whether they were true or untrue! Through my extensive counseling practice, I had untold opportunities to confirm my observation that belief was the key. *Our lives are the manifestations that arise from the beliefs and feelings of self-worth we establish in our lives as causes.*

Based upon this realization, I conclude that the magic wand, the "open sesame" of life is, indeed, the art of being yourself. Come home to your spiritual base, where the real you originated: Perfect Cause, Perfect Man/Woman, Perfect Being.

Emerson succinctly stated, "To imitate is suicide." Why? Because imitation is a powerful statement that you believe someone else has more to offer to life than you. When you abdicate your own expression, you are committing a form of suicide. As you develop the art of being your spiritually-empowered, dynamic self, your successes will come as easily as day follows night.

You have no equal.

Chapter One

~~~

An Unfinished Masterpiece

Ninety-eight percent of us die before we taste the nectar of our own magnificence.

—Abraham Maslow

~~~

Man's mind, once stretched by a new idea, never regains its original dimensions.

—Oliver Wendell Holmes

One of the most beautiful, challenging, and rewarding pursuits of life is the art of being yourself—not just your personality self, but your real self. Why? Your real self is so dynamic, so scintillating, so exquisitely unique that it defies all of your pre-existing concepts or imaginings! An exciting exploration lies ahead for you when you begin the journey of self-discovery. Getting to know *you* and the reality of your being can be the most fulfilling experience of your life.

In order for us to expand our capacity in any direction—mentally, physically, socially, economically—we need to connect with the spiritual nature of our being. We must know that we stem from Reality, the Truth, the All That Is. This knowing opens the channels through which divine inspiration flows into our stream of consciousness. When we try to make it alone, whatever we accomplish is not lasting. When we relate to the Source, we are tied in with an infinite power and become powerful instruments for higher expression.

We all have our being in the same Source, yet each of us is individual. It is not fair to compare ourselves to Tom, Dick, Harry, Susie, or anyone else. We can appreciate their abilities and talents. We can honor their way of expressing life, but we must recognize that we have just as direct a line to truth as they do. If they seem to be expressing more abundantly than we, it is because they are keeping their line of communication with the Source open.

In order for us to be aware of our connection with the Whole and to express from the spiritual nature within us, we need to recognize that we must make choices and that as we make choices our lives change. We always have the power to make choices, and the power we have is ever present with us. We do not have to wait until tomorrow. Today is the moment we choose the life we will live.

Instead of struggling alone to improve the conditions of our lives, there is a better way, and that is the way that Jesus taught us two thousand years ago: "Seek ye first the kingdom." In the language of today, we would call the "kingdom" the key to infinite wisdom and spiritual enlightenment. Why is it so important to seek this kingdom? When we gain spiritual enlightenment and wisdom, all the improvements we desire in our life flow naturally. We do not have to struggle and strain. They come to us as a natural part of our inheritance as spiritual beings in an earthly experience.

This does not mean that we fold our hands and wait for Spirit to do everything for us, but it does mean that our connection with Spirit—our conscious connection with it—makes everything easier to attain on every level of our living, for there is always the flow of power to fortify our outer efforts.

Never, then, compare yourself with anyone else. You are an individual in your own right. Decide that you will find the point of power within you and be the self you were meant to be. You do not have to tear someone else down to build yourself up, nor do you have to build someone else up and think you are less able to accomplish than he or she. It is not a matter of one person being more capable than another. It is a matter of expressing the unique quality of you, yourself, that should concern you. If you are exercising infinite wisdom and not just the knowledge of the finite mind and senses, you will realize the infinite beauty and capability, as well as the uniqueness, of each and every unit of life and the importance of each not imitating another but simply striving to be itself, himself, or herself.

Somewhere, sometime, you will be compelled by the urge within you to make decisions about your own life. The push within you will become so great that you will know it is time for you to take another step in consciousness. It will be time for you to evolve into a new, higher level of beingness. That time could be today, for if you are reading this message, you are already seeking—and what you are seeking lies right within your own consciousness.

Begin now to exercise your divine right. Affirm:

1. *I am the builder of my own life. No one else can build it for me.*
2. *I decide to be myself, my real self.*
3. *I decide to enlarge my capacity for living in all area.*
4. *I achieve this expansion by becoming consciously aware that the reality of my true self is spiritual and that I always have access to the spiritual power within me.*
5. *I surge ahead to newness by keeping my spiritual channel open at all times.*

Do not look around you for endorsement or approval. Look within yourself. See your unlimited potential, your boundless capacity, and determine to express them. You are not dependent upon outward approval, but you are dependent upon deciding to be your real self. Until you make that decision, you will not have your own inner approval and that is what counts.

Sometimes we know that we must make a decision to move in one direction or another, yet we find ourselves sitting astride the fence of indecision. In this state we are using a great deal of energy and getting nowhere. We just sit there in frustration, which is like sitting on dynamite, for sooner or later an explosion will force a decision that we could have made of our own accord.

You are a part of the principle of reality. You are a part of a beautiful consciousness, an infinite mind, a storehouse of original ideas, but you have to be the one to decide how and when you will respond to what you are and what you have. Do not say, "My children or my job make too many demands upon me," or "I must talk it over with my spouse before I make a decision about my own life."

If you do that, there will always be someone or something or some condition or situation that will deter you. You must reach your own point of decision. When you get sick and tired of being sick and tired, you will decide to do something about it. When you see that you are basing your indecision on something other than yourself, you will know you must take action.

Why not say to yourself today:

I have decided to be happy. I have decided to be successful. I have decided to decide what is important about the living of my own life. I have decided to touch the inner consciousness of my being, to become acquainted with my real self and to express this self. I have decided to be joyous in the living of this life. Being my real self is not dependent upon any person, place or thing. It is dependent only upon my own consciousness, my own contact with inner reality. I seek first the kingdom, knowing that all else needed for a full, happy and abundant life will be added unto me. This I decide today, this moment.

As you make your decisions about your own life, everything else will begin to fall into place. Living from the real self of you is the key that unlocks all the doors of your consciousness and makes all things possible for you. The only barrier between you and your good, between you and your real self, is your own mind. When you can let go of analyzing, separating, and trying to reason everything out, and turn your thoughts inward in a receptive manner, you will begin to feel, know and experience things you could not figure out with your finite mind in a thousand years.

The Bible says, "In quietness and confidence is your strength," and I say that in this quietness and confidence, you will find not only your strength, but also the real nature of your being, and expressing this beingness will become a joy and a privilege.

A New Beginning

Each moment in time is an opportunity to ascend in consciousness and become aware of the power that is ever present within you. You do not have to wait for a special day like Easter, Christmas, or New Year's to experience a new beginning. Each day of your life is a special day, a special opportunity to let the glory of Spirit shine through you.

Let us feel a genuine happiness that lights us up from within. Let us not just think about this happiness, but experience it and know that it is the higher self within expressing through us. Any special day, and *this* is a special day, is for the purpose of focusing our attention on the reality of our being and triggering the joy and love that are within us.

When we experience something, we express that something. It flows through us and out into our world. We cannot, then, come into a new consciousness without its showing forth in our everyday life. We cannot be lifted up in consciousness without that experience affecting, in a measure, everyone with whom we come in contact. It is like perfume—you cannot enjoy it without the fragrance spilling over upon others.

Know that within you is your own spark of divinity, making you one with essential power and one with all humanity. Know that it is this Life within you that gives you life and being, and that your awareness of it will enable you to throw off all limitations, will enable you to turn away from all false appearances, will resurrect your life and lift you in consciousness.

Regardless of what you have gone through, regardless of how things appear on the surface, here is the most beautiful opportunity to experience a new beginning. When this new beginning comes to you, it will be in the flash of the moment, and it can be *this* moment, if you are ready to let go of all your resistance and simply accept wholeheartedly what you already know deep within.

You are not just human. You are divine, and I am sure you accept this mentally, but do you really *believe* it; do you really *feel* it; do you really *accept* it? When you do, you will know intuitively that you and the Infinite Presence are one and that all that the Creator has is yours. You will know that one cycle of your life is finished and that a new one has begun. You will feel a new surge of life and you will know that you have made a breakthrough to a higher dimension of consciousness. That's what spiritual science is all about. It is doing us no good if it does not inspire us to complete one cycle of our lives and make a breakthrough into a higher dimension, if it does not constantly open new doors to us and new avenues to be explored.

The true message of any philosophical thought is not just to teach us to live better and more moral lives, but to lead us back in consciousness to our Source, to the infinite riches of Spirit. When this realization or breakthrough comes, we see ourselves as a completely different entity or being. We have a new identity, and the whole world takes on a different aspect.

When the realization of your divinity comes to you, you know that you are eternal. You know that you never had a beginning and that you will never have an end. You know that this world is only one little spot where your consciousness appears to be residing in a physical body at this time, and that there are worlds without end for you to experience—in which to grow. What an exalted and expanded feeling that is! I believe the time will come when we will step across the boundary of one world into another without the process called death. Actually, the boundary line is only in our imagination anyway, like the boundary line of states and nations on a map.

We all know that this world, beautiful as it is, is not enough. There is something in each of us that is crying out forever to be free and we are not satisfied with any limitation. This is why we want to grow and expand. This is why we are never satisfied. The more we get, the more we want, and all the time what we want goes far beyond anything we can possess, like money. Sometimes we spend most of a lifetime before we realize there is something more we need, and that something more is reunion with the Spirit within us.

Why go on seeking light and life in things? Remember Jesus said to the weeping women, "Why seek ye the living among the dead?" If you make contact with the spiritual power within you, you will have all the things you need and you will have health and love, for these are a natural result of the spiritual life.

Come to the realization today, right now, both in mind and heart, that you are throwing off, completely eliminating from your consciousness, all that has gone before this minute. New ways are opening up before you that you have not known before. New possibilities make themselves known to you.

Just as the sun comes out gloriously at the dawn of each new day and the darkness melts away, so will the inner darkness melt away as your consciousness yields to light and more light. Darkness cannot wrestle with light. It can do nothing but yield.

What happens when the light comes and the darkness is dispelled? There is a revelation. Things are revealed that could never be seen in the darkness. Things we stumbled against before are seen clearly and can be avoided. That which appeared forbidding and frightening, when seen in the light, now holds no fear for us.

When the light comes to your consciousness, all the dark areas in your life are cleared away. There are no shadows left. There is no place in the light of Truth for darkness and negation. Say, then, to yourself, "I am the light. I am the light and there is no darkness."

It is a marvelous thing that everything that comes into the light is transformed or revealed in its true estate. Sickness disappears, lack disappears, and fears fade away. Whenever anything enters into your consciousness or comes close to you that begins to place you in a shadow of negativity, at that moment recognize: "I am the light. I am the light and the light dispels the darkness."

This moment is the best moment of your life to experience your illumined self and to go forth and express it.

10

You Are Spirit Expressing

You are the beloved of the Most High, but to be the beautiful individual you were intended to be, you must search deep within and behold the tabernacle of the Most High. Beautiful individuals blossom from beautiful thoughts and beautiful thoughts come only from the originating Mind of Spirit. Each of us has the ability to weave a beautiful tapestry of our lives, if we accept these thoughts from Universal Mind as our thoughts.

When we are troubled from within, it soon becomes outside trouble. That is why we must reach deep within and open our consciousness and make contact with the great Reservoir, the great indwelling Presence within us. This glorious Presence will fire our imagination with wonder and beauty. We need, then, meditation, affirmative prayer and communion with the Presence within in order to feel a sense of oneness and belongingness.

Light is needed today possibly more than at any other time in the history of the world. We are seeking this spiritual light today. Our desire to bring electrical light wherever there is physical darkness into cities, homes and public places but dimly reflects the urgency within us to bring more spiritual light into our consciousness. To find this light, we must turn within and commune with the Presence that knows itself as itself, that knows the glory and the power and the stature of our being. The stature of every individual—that is, spiritual stature—is inconceivably great. We must begin to reflect this greatness in our everyday living.

Many individuals, when some innovation is put into effect, say: "Oh, I thought of that a long time ago!" Well, then, why didn't they do something about it? "Oh, I didn't think I was able to." This is a great problem...the lack of faith we have in ourselves. We don't trust ourselves enough. We lack strong convictions regarding ourselves. We need to feel that no one is really against us, that everyone is for us, that this whole universe is a play of things working together for good. Once we erase the belief in our consciousness that Tom, Dick, Harry or Susie are against us, we come into a unifying consciousness that this is indeed a friendly universe.

Spiritual ideas are eager to come to you, but you are not receptive to them if you are depressed. Lift yourself into the light of your true being. Spiritual ideas are not freely available to people who are bankrupt in their thoughts regarding themselves. Spiritual ideas cannot come through people who attach no value to themselves.

Spiritual ideas can, on the other hand, come through and make your greatness shine forth when you recognize that you are much more than flesh. You are the essence of life itself. You are the dignity of Divine Mind expressing here. Spirit within is constantly nudging you to greater expressions of wholeness, but if you dwell in morbidity or depression or negation—if you insist upon holding and hugging close to you everything that is tinged with fear and doubt—you let yourself be robbed of the beauty and dignity of life, and you never know your true nature.

The moment you elevate yourself in consciousness to your true estate, that moment you are in command of the forces and power within you. They are within you right now, waiting for you to assume command. When you do, you will live from the true center of your own being and be the master of your own words and your own actions.

Come out and play the game of life. There is a divine plan for you and for everyone, and that divine plan is one of freedom, but freedom is something to be experienced—not a word to be said with the lips only. We experience this freedom through understanding and cooperation with Universal Law.

Decay sets in when we fail to fully participate in life. There is a vast difference between existing from Monday to Friday and really living. There is much more to life than just getting by. When we let ourselves be caught in the rut of dull routine, we are not open to the freshness and airiness of life. We cannot thrive in a tightly closed container. We must be free in the light. If thoughts are shutting you away from life, take command over them. If fears plague you, take command over them. Take command over any and all petty ideas that rob you of the true identity and dignity of your beingness, and eradicate them.

The Divine Presence expresses by means of us. Infinite Intelligence did not create lack or limitation, but we limit our own life. We have conditioned ourselves to many kinds of thinking—much of which is not favorable to the abundant life. Some people actually believe that a deity created poverty and that some benevolent dictator favors them when they experience poverty with resignation!

Nothing could be further from the truth. As long as we condition ourselves to the negative side of things, we cannot enjoy the life more abundant of which Jesus spoke. This abundant life is right at hand—just as the fields were ripe to harvest—but we must accept this truth before we can experience it. Universal Law is the law of good and it takes our self-acceptance—not what others may think of us, but our own self-acceptance—to experience this good.

Today let us come into the realization of the dignity of the Spirit within us—the dignity and wonder and greatness with which Mind endowed us. In Spirit and in Truth, we all live, move and have our being. Let us today elevate our consciousness to the dignity of our true beingness. The dignity of our true being is Infinite Intelligence in action.

Dreams

Every one of us has a dream for the future, and we all handle our dreams in one of two ways. Some dream and dream and dream, and dream again, but do nothing else. Others dream and act out their dreams. They set about making their dreams come true. Then they dream new dreams and bring those new dreams into reality.

Both vision and action are important. The Bible tells us, "Where there is no vision, the people perish." And we might add: "Where there is no action, the dream goes no place and does nothing." So, both vision and action supplement each other. Thus, we must dream our dreams. We must have our vision, but we cannot stop there. We must begin to *feel* our dream. We must be sensitive to our dream with every sense we have—and we must implant it so deeply and strongly in our consciousness that it becomes powerful enough to move us to action. To merely dream without performance is of no value at all.

Have your dreams. Let hope rise high within your breast. Keep your vision clear—but remember you cannot stop there. Your dreams tell you what you want in life. They tell you what you need in order to fulfill your life—what is good for you—but you must do more than think about them. You must act.

Of course, it is easier to dream about a brave new world of our own than it is to do something about it. One reason we hesitate to act is that we let fears and doubt crowd in and make our dreams murky. We let things plague us—tear us apart— destroy us—divide us—keep us keyed up—keep us in chaos, because of those fears and doubts.

What can we do to remedy this? We can sit right down in the confines of our own consciousness and meet this situation head on. We will find, when we stand up to fear, that there is nothing to substantiate it. There is no law that upholds or stands back of negativity. Yet, as long as we let fears and doubts infest our consciousness, they infect greater and greater areas of our livingness. We find ourselves a prey to all kinds of negative suggestion that come along.

Granted you may have many fears, many doubts, many uncertainties. Whatever they are, begin to say to yourself: "All right. I have these fears and doubts, but I am going to work this out in my own consciousness, in my own mind, because I know I control my own circumstances. They can do to me only what I permit them to do. I am not a body containing a mind, but infinite Spirit, infinite love using a body."

Do not allow negative parasites to eat away at your dreams. Go into your mind and clear them out. Make peace with yourself. You have the power to meet all circumstances, to overcome all difficulties, when you meet them in the consciousness of truth. This is actually the only place you can meet anything—in consciousness. By doing this, you can make your dreams become realities and you can wipe out the nightmarish ones that repeat themselves over and over again.

The Science of Mind teaches that each of us controls our circumstances. We control our thinking and our actions. In this way, we can move to make our dreams come true. We know we have the power within to aid us the moment we begin to move forward constructively.

The will to succeed and live must become the dominating will in our lives. When that is greater than the will to fail, we will not only dream our dreams, but we will also move to bring them to fruition.

Some of us hesitate when faced with challenges. Everything that is great and on top is always challenged—everything.

You may remember Man of War. He was on top. He was the greatest race horse of his time. In one particular race, he was running beautifully with another horse. The first quarter they were together and at the second quarter they were together. They were still together at the third quarter. Suddenly, the jockey on Man of War realized he had to do something.

Now, Man of War had never had a whip used on him. He and his jockey were as one. The jockey did not know what to do, but he felt that this was a time to use the whip. He did. Man of War was so shocked that he shot out and moved seven lengths ahead of the other horses.

In our own lives, we will find that we need challenges and sometimes shocks to move us to action. If we have an inferiority complex, we cannot meet the challenges that urge us on. We must rely on Something within us to aid us. The horse that lost the race with Man of War never ran again. He never challenged another horse—yet, he was good or he could not have stayed abreast Man of War for three-quarters of the race. Perhaps, he developed a defeated attitude—an inferiority complex!

No matter what challenges you—if you find that you don't make it the first time, have the intelligence to get right back in the race again. Have the will to succeed, the will to win, the will to perform by using this great Something within you. You will find yourself moving to the top. You will find yourself succeeding. You will know what it is to have your dreams come true when you know there is a Power within you greater than you are, and you can use it.

Today, dream that impossible dream—and make it possible by putting it into action. All the forces of Life will move with you, to make your dream come true.

Free Yourself from Limitation

Know there is that within you which supports you in every regard. Know you are not hampered by outside appearances because you have a mind within you that is infinite. You have a spirit within you that is unlimited. You have a Presence within you that is all-loving.

Live life drawing from powerful resources at the center of your being, and you will know the truth—that you are completely unlimited in every manner and that you cannot be locked in or blocked in any area of your living. Knowing this will enhance your living and free you to express at your optimum.

Many times, without knowing it consciously, we put limitations upon the Infinite. We do this when we put restrictions upon ourselves. We should not create boundaries or limitations. Infinite Spirit does not impose limitations upon us. Our limitations are self-imposed.

See yourself in a completely new light today. Realize that there is no need for you to live life as a prisoner. You should live life as a great adventurer, always ready to discover more and more. You can quickly discern just how you feel about life if you will take time to ask yourself some questions and disclose some of your attitudes.

Ask yourself today, "What is my attitude about myself? What is my attitude about life generally? What is my attitude about people I meet? Is my attitude hinged on the concept that all advancement is outside of myself?" As you mull over these few questions, others will come quickly to mind. This exercise can be very enlightening, for often we go on from day to day taking for granted that life as we experience it is the way it has to be.

Within you is a glorious life force which puts no restrictions upon you. The blueprint of you is so great that you can spend eons of time getting to know yourself in actuality as you are in potential. However, if you get caught in repression and suppression, you will not know this greater you. You will not feel free.

We get caught in certain mental attitudes, and they impede our growth. We acquire fixed, set, cut-and-dried opinions. We become crystallized, and often we are completely unaware of this. It is important to examine our ideas and beliefs from time to time to be sure we are not becoming crystallized and set in any area of our thinking.

A few of the fixed ideas we all indulge in from time to time relate to our health, our progress in life, our age, and our opportunities. We assume it is too late to do anything about ourselves. This is a false idea, yet we let this erroneous belief become ensconced in our thinking to rob us of motivation and self-esteem.

Try this experiment: Think of today as the first day of your life. It is a completely new beginning. You have no set ideas. You have no hang-ups. You are not crystallized in any manner. You are freshly born. It is a new day and you are new in it. Can you get a glimmer of what this would be like? Well, it can be like that all the time if you choose it to be. Think each day of what you would like to do and be if you were freshly born and living the first day of your life with no impediments of any kind. It can prove very profitable to you, for if you think consistently in a positive, constructive way, positive and constructive things will show forth in your experience.

Some people like to be set in their ideas, for they do not like to make the effort to change. You might as well try to move the Rock of Gibraltar as to move them to newness, but I am sure you are not of that caliber. If you were, you would not be reading this book. You would have no interest in it.

Say to yourself today:

I am growing each day. I am growing each moment. I am growing in knowledge. I am growing in understanding. I am growing in love. I am growing in ideas.

You have heard people say, "I wish I were a kid again so I could grow up better." Well, you are still young in spirit. Each undertaking you pursue finds you young and ready to grow. With every project, newness causes your expansion and growing maturity. Do not look backward and wish, look forward and exult in the joyous experiences ahead of you. People who look backward have not moved toward maturity. They are still yearning for the status quo of the infant. Infancy, however, brings you to a state of helplessness.

In the physical world everything must grow or die. That is true of plants, trees, flowers, animals, and it is also true of the physical body. Growth is a continuous process of unfoldment into something more than is evident at the present moment. It is First Cause itself expressing through its creation. It is life and movement and ongoingness. We often say that the nature of Universal Intelligence is changeless, but this does not mean that Mind is static, for Divine Mind is ever active, ever creative.

Inwardly you will never stop growing. Outwardly, you may become sluggish, stale, or dull. You may lose your zest for living. You may feel boxed in. You may feel stuck, hampered, impeded, restricted, set and fixed. Yet Life is just as active as it always was and is always inviting you to participate in the feast of living.

Know today that there is Something within you that is desirous of revealing itself through you. As it reveals itself through you, you know spiritual self-revelation. You know a newness of consciousness. You know you are not dependent upon people "out there." You are not dependent upon everyone else's opinions. You know that there is a center of truth within you and that as you acknowledge it and let it express through you, you will continue to grow and unfold according to the big blueprint of you, becoming more each day of what you potentially are.

Let this be the first day of your life—a new beginning for you, free of everything that might heretofore have hampered you or held you back. Be free, fresh, and new with the newness of Spirit.

Chapter Two

~~~

You Are Here
for a Reason

The question is asked, if life's journey be endless, where is its goal. The answer is, it is everywhere. We are in a palace which has no end, but which we have reached.

–Rabindranath Tagore

~~~

The great and glorious masterpiece of man is how to live with a purpose.

–Michel de Montaigne

Each of us should sense deep within ourselves that our existence is perfect and whole and that there is a purpose for us to fulfill in this life. No matter how numerous or diverse our goals, our main purpose is to grow in every area of our being. To grow, we must use the intelligence and the potential within us. We always grow from the inside out, like the unfolding of a rose.

If you do not know what your specific purpose is, you can know that growing is certainly the principal one. You are Life in action. You cannot remain static any more than Life itself can. Activity has to take place and every activity must have a result. The result depends upon your purpose, the direction in which you focus your activity.

Everything in life seems to be moving toward an end result, yet when that end result is reached, another stretches out beyond it. We are forever moving forward. We can achieve this movement in a dynamic and purposeful way, or we can just wander aimlessly along, missing out on the fulfilling spiritual, mental and emotional benefits of growth.

Say to yourself right now:

My life is a dynamic experience. The creative mind expresses creatively by means of me. Everything I undertake succeeds through my dynamic approach.

When you begin to really feel the truth of this affirmation, you will see Universal Law working with infinite energy. Think, "Infinite energy is expressing itself by means of me." Know that an unlimited Source is constantly supplying you with energy all the time.

Each of us will meet life in our own fashion, for while we are all equal, we approach life in many different ways. All of us are constantly ascending the spiral of life. Some dawdle along the way, some take many detours, and others go purposefully toward their goals.

Feel that you are supplied with infinite energy which never runs out. You do not have to run a marathon in order to prove you have this dynamic energy. Just feel it flowing through you in all the activities of your day. See yourself as whole. See yourself as part of the Universal Intelligence. Know that you are never depleted of this vital flow of life, because you are a part of All That Is.

The Infinite created you to be of service to yourself, to your world and to others. The Infinite created you to succeed. Losers were never born. They are made somewhere along the way, and as long as you can know that Life created every individual to succeed, you will move toward your goal, a winner.

Get a new subjective pattern within your consciousness. You were born to win, born to be healthy, born to experience the goodness of the universe. When you move yourself into this consciousness, you cannot fail. Your feet will move in the right direction. Your hands will perform the right tasks, and your mind will be involved in the right plans to bring out the best that is within you.

Many times we hear people say, "I was born without this and I was born without that." They have a consciousness of being without. They magnify the without, until it becomes their subjective state of mind. The vital force within us can be used to bring us good or ill. We pour it into molds of our own making and then experience what we have formed.

When you first attempt to turn within you might ask, "But what am I turning in toward?" Begin to feel that you are drawing upon a vital force that is within you. You are attuning yourself to a Power, a dynamic force of creativity. Like turning on the faucet and expecting water to come out, when you turn within, you are expecting the flow of Spirit.

If you press a button on an electric stove, the grill will get hot. If you turn the gas jet on, a flame appears. Now, when you turn within, expect to find something. Expect to find the vital force of life, the Power that is within you. Have a consciousness of expectancy.

If you turn within expecting to sense something, to contact the Power that is always available, then something will begin to come through. You will begin to feel your connection with the flow of life within you.

I am sure none of us live as vitally as we could. I am sure none of us uses our wisdom to the greatest advantage and thereby experiences the best that we could. Life is not lived in length of years but in the intensity of our experiencing it—the degree to which we embrace it wholeheartedly.

Jesus said, "Seek and ye shall find." In the light of our understanding today, we could say, "Accept and it shall be yours." All things await our acceptance in the great storehouse of Mind. They are within our own consciousness. You do not have to chase something and feel that it is running away from you. Stand still, expand your consciousness of what you desire, and accept it.

The vital side of life is invisible. We see only the effects of its vitality. We do not see the wind, but we feel it and we see how it affects the trees, the plants, or anything that it touches. The same thing is true of you. The most important part of you, the vital part, is invisible. We need to dig deeply within ourselves and come to know ourselves better.

Most of us are strangers to the beauty and intelligence within us. It is only when we can feel we are communicating, reaching within and bringing forth more of ourselves that we can know this vital force within us. It is always wanting to give us more. It is always wanting to let more of Reality express through us.

Say to yourself:

I cease to seek for the fulfillment of my desires among things. I look within and join myself in consciousness with the vital force of Life itself. I let more of reality express through me today.

Life Is Always Giving to You

The whole basis of the Science of Mind rests upon the principle that the mind you are using is Universal Mind. *There is no other mind.* You are the Divine in expression. You are the image and likeness of Infinite Perfection. You are both Adam and Eve, the intellect and the intuition.

You are no longer in the Garden of Eden of consciousness where everything was provided at an instinctual level. You are a thinking, choosing, creative individual who operates from the power within. Adam and Eve represent what we call the conscious and the subconscious mind. The conscious mind is the selector. The subconscious mind, the receptor, acts out that which you select.

This is why the consciousness of Truth can set you free. You are the only one who denies your own good. When you realize the Truth for yourself, you will know that you are the right person, in the right place, at the right time, doing the right thing. It could not be otherwise, for consciousness always creates after its own nature.

Know today that health is a divine right; sickness is humanly created. You can never "lose" your health. Never. If you ever lost your health, where do you think you would find it? Under the bed? In a closet? Or did it go down the street to somebody else? If you ever think, "I'm losing my health," you are thinking incorrectly. No matter how ill you may be, you could never experience health again if you did not have it within you all the time. It is there all the time.

Even if you should physically die, you have not lost your health. You are really Mind, spiritual consciousness manifesting itself in body. You can never lose anything that is yours by divine right. Is the sun lost when hidden for a time behind a cloud? You will always continue to exist, although you will always be challenged to change and to advance.

The perfection of Spirit, which knows no duality whatsoever, is always at the basis of your being. What you outpicture depends upon your state of consciousness. Doctors cannot heal us. They can remove obstructions; they can set bones; they can relieve a condition, but the Power within must heal. If sickness were real and permanent, if it were the true nature of your being, then nothing could make you experience health; but if health is the true nature of being, when you remove blinders

27

from your eyes and see the truth, you experience your true birthright.

When you are experiencing poverty, your mind is closed to the abundance all around you. If you are absolutely confused, you must realize that at the very center of your confusion, in the center or "eye" of the hurricane, is the answer, which is: Where there seems to be discord, there is peace; where there seems to be hatred, there is love. The negative attitudes are only an inverse view of that which is real.

We are dealing with a science here. The science that Jesus taught us in the language of two thousand years ago is the same science Ernest Holmes gave us in the language of today. The Bible says, "As a man thinketh in his heart, so is he." All right. You want to change your life and change it for the better. How do you do it? Where do you begin?

You change your life by changing your thoughts, degree by degree, thought replacing thought. Thoughts are things and things are result of thoughts. Everything outpictured was first an idea in Mind. All that you see or can sense in any fashion is the result of an idea that began in Mind and outpictured objectively. This is why by changing your thought, you can change your life for the better.

Begin today to exercise your divine birthright. Realize that your abundance is within you; your health is within you; your peace is within you—all despite appearances. Remember Jesus said that we are not to look at appearances. When we do, we give them power. However, that does not mean that we sweep them under a rug.

We have a marvelous consciousness within us and we must work with ourselves. Each of us is a law unto our own being. The Truth is within us, but if we insist upon focusing on appearances and believing in a nontruth, this is what we will experience. It is like taking pictures. We get what is impressed on the film of mind.

Spirit does not arbitrarily give and take. What appears to be taken from us is in reality an action resulting from a conscious or subconscious acceptance within us. Spirit is a giver. Spirit is the infinite giver and that Infinite Giver is everywhere present.

Spirit does not give with the idea of teasing us or taking away from us, but with the idea of creating a better universe. Say to yourself today:

> *I am the right person in consciousness today. Where I go from today depends entirely upon me. It depends upon how I use the consciousness within me. I can go on in the same old rut or I can make my life new and promising. When I change my thought, when I change my ideas, when I give up my old concepts, my life changes for the better. This I do today and claim that which is mine by divine right. I ignore appearances and consciously choose what I want to outpicture.*

Weave the Life You Want Through Prayer

Suppose right in front of you this day, there is a loom. Attached to this loom is the yarn with which to weave. There you are, the weaver, sitting before the loom. You are going to weave your own pattern of life on the loom, and no one else can do this for you. You are the weaver of your life pattern.

If you choose to weave a design that is not attractive to you, you cannot, upon looking at the finished product, say, "Look at what the loom did!" You can't blame Aunt Sophie, can you? The loom is absolutely impersonal. That loom will take whatever you weave into it and the yarn will take the shape of that which you give it.

Suppose you look at what you have woven up to this point. Don't continue to weave a mistake into it if the pattern is not to your liking. You can change it right now. You are the weaver. You weave into your life your thoughts, your opinions, your ideas, your feelings, your reactions, your own interpretations. Universal Law is like the loom. It is absolutely impersonal. It doesn't say to you, "Look, you have dropped a stitch." No, the Universe is absolutely impersonal. We personalize the impersonal. It takes what you weave into it and gives you the result of your weaving. If you weave an undesirable pattern, life is not at fault, nor is the loom.

Since you are the weaver and the loom is right there before you, you have the right to weave your life and make it something that can be a great asset to you.

"How," you may ask, "can I be sure that my pattern is appropriate?" Look within and know that Spirit made you immortal and eternal. Spirit made you in its own image and likeness, which is unseen; the creative thinker, divine potential, ever forming the fabric of life out of universal substance everywhere present. Each individual is forever in the consciousness of Spirit, so the consciousness of Spirit is in the individual. You may be sure, then, that no matter what you are going through—regardless of what surrounds you—the perfect state of your being always was and will be.

How can you begin to weave this perfection into the pattern of your life on your loom? One way is through affirmative prayer, or spiritual mind treatment. Affirmative prayer is not an intellectual petition. People sometimes pray as if they were intellectually trying to bribe an arbitrary deity. "God, you do this for me, and I will do that for you." No, there is no bribery in affirmative prayer. There is intelligence and deep feeling, actually a realization of the creative ability within you. You expect this creativity to work out through you according to the degree to which you can see and feel the perfect pattern.

Affirmative prayer is active communion. Just as a weaver's hand communes with the thread as it weaves a pattern on the loom, so in affirmative prayer you commune with the creative Power within you, which is warm and colorful, vital and sparkling. Unless you can see in your mind the pattern or design you want to put on the loom, you will have a hodgepodge of color. The same thing is true of prayer—your thoughts and words and feelings need to embody that which you desire in order to bring it forth.

When you weave a pattern on your loom, you already know what the design is to be. If you didn't, there would be no starting point. To weave beautifully, you must see a beautiful design. To live beautifully, you must realize that the perfect individual, made from the beginning of time, is already within and waiting to manifest in your life.

Even if a person you meet tomorrow is a thorn in your side, the perfect nature of being abides within that individual. You must steadily maintain your oneness with the divine Source and recognize it in others, not for what they are doing, but for what they *are*—perfect, spiritual, and divine. That is how you have to see life. See it in a consciousness of Truth and right action.

Years will not necessarily develop your weaving skill. Age is not necessarily an indicator of maturity and wisdom. It depends upon what kind of weaving you have been doing throughout the years. If you are still using the same old thought-pattern and the same old thread and the same old methods you were using many years ago, how much have you learned about the designing of a beautiful life?

Experience is not necessarily a productive teacher. Experience may only teach us to do the same thing in the same way.

Infinite Intelligence within you is the real teacher. It teaches you new ideas, new approaches. This is the teacher you should commune with—not experience.

Ideas do not come from experience. Ideas create experience. So do not depend on experience to bring new ideas to you. Newness comes through you. Experience, wonderful as it may be—good, bad, or indifferent—doesn't necessarily teach a lesson. Have you not met individuals who have experienced the same thing over and over and over again? Have they learned? If they had, would they be repeating the same old pattern?

As you sit before your loom today, behold the design you want to weave. Behold that which you are; behold the Presence, the Power, and the Love within you. Know that you are not your name, you are not flesh, you are an expression of Spirit. You are Life. You are an individual being governed by divine Love. You are an individual made of the substance of Truth.

Determine that these are the things with which you are going to color and vitalize the weaving on your loom. You are motivated from the center out. You are governed and directed from within. Come to your loom in this consciousness. You are the weaver of your life. Create on your loom a beautiful, new design for living today.

Your Greatest Desire

If you find that certain areas in your life are not to your liking, begin a program right now to change them. Begin by examining your whole attitude, your whole feeling, your whole idea of life and yourself and be willing to change what needs changing. Begin to identify with the reality of your being.

What a transformation would take place for all of us if we

could come into a new awareness today. We would go about the living of our lives with a new consciousness. We would see new opportunities. We would experience wholeness, peace and harmony. We would be able to use the inspiration and divine Intelligence which are native to all of us.

Close your eyes for a moment and in your mind's eye see a tightly closed flower bud. Then, see this bud begin to open and unfold. Watch it as each petal is loosened and folded back, until you begin to see the golden center. Now transpose this flower into the idea of consciousness and feel your consciousness open and unfold until you find your golden center. Of course, consciousness will be ever-unfolding, but this exercise will give you a feeling of that process taking place.

If you are coming into a new awareness, you know that the transformation brings within it the solution to your problem. You can consider the problem solved. Illness is diminishing and health is becoming manifest. Lack is finished and the flow of abundance is coming into being.

When you look in the mailbox, the bills will still be there. This is no magic trick. No fairy godmother is going to wave a wand and presto! all is changed. No, it is not as easy as that. What I am talking about is the changing of consciousness in such a way that you have a health consciousness, an abundance conscious-ness, and a Truth consciousness, instead of the faulty way you had of looking at things. When the change takes place in consciousness, then your good will begin to flow. It will begin to manifest in your outer life.

I believe this is what Jesus meant when he said, "Ye must be born again." When the rich young man asked, "How can I enter my mother's womb and be born again?" Jesus said, "You must be born of the water and the spirit." The mind and the emotions must be reborn. Everything must be seen in a new and different light.

Somewhere, sometime in your life, you and you alone must give birth to the real you. You and you alone must awaken your consciousness. You and you alone must begin to see that you are dealing with a limitless power, with a principle which operates by an exact law. You must realize the presence of Perfection within you. You cannot be constructive one minute and negative the next moment. You must stand on a firm foundation of spiritual principle.

You can readily see how impossible it is for the subconscious mind to give you what you want if one moment you think in terms of success and the next in terms of failure. You can readily see that you are not giving it a chance if one moment you think in terms of illness and in the next in terms of health. No. There have to be firm commitments supported by disciplined thinking if you want the right results.

What is it you desire? What is it that you desire with all your heart, with all your mind, and with all your soul? I know everyone has several desires, but pick the strongest one you have. Pick the one you feel is the most important to you. After you have done that, say, "This is what I desire more than anything else in my whole life." Then begin to think in the direction of your desire. Do not waver back and forth. Do not think of all the obstacles in the way. Do not let confusion enter in. Do not become irritated because it is not fulfilled as though by a bolt out of the blue.

Keep your mind steady on the goal. Keep your emotions positive and firm, supportive and focused. Keep repositioning yourself in mind and your desire will become a manifestation. Remember that what you feel and what you think, you become. Think yourself into a whole new consciousness. Enter into a new thought, a new idea, and a new image of yourself.

Perhaps you look at your life and say, "My whole life has

been one big problem after another, one failure after another. I have experienced nothing but failure." With this attitude you should be the most successful failure on the face of the earth. You are dwelling consistently on the past, identifying emotionally with failure and releasing these erroneous images into Universal Law, which never questions the veracity of what you give it. It simply accepts the data and produces. What must you do? You must cease dwelling on the past and failure and think just the opposite. You must think on success. You must know that failure is not native to you, but success is. You must remember that you are the captain and the director of your life. You must realize that the Presence is within you and that it does not know such a thing as failure.

Remember: What you desire with all your heart, with all your mind, with all your soul, you will become—if you believe it and commit your thoughts and energies to its attainment. If you are not becoming it, then there must be something within you that does not want it as much as you think you do, or maybe you want it, but negate the manifestation by believing that it is impossible for you to attain.

Today, direct the Power within you to express through you the best ideas, the best ways, the best methods, the best expressions, and the best consciousness. Know what you desire of Life. Do not ask someone else, "What do you think I ought to do? What do you think I should desire? What do you think would be the best thing in the world for me?" No one can tell you that except yourself. What other people think you ought to do—the "if I were you"—is mere conjecture, because they are not you. The richest guidance you can follow is found intuitively within.

I ask you to inquire, "If I had but one opportunity for a single desire to be granted, what is it that I want more than anything else in the world?" When you decide, keep that desire before you. Feed it with your thoughts, your feelings, and your beliefs. Let it become a law unto your being. Your total acceptance of it will be acted upon by your subconscious, and you will see results.

If you turn back, if you waver back and forth, if you doubt, or if you fear, what you desire to experience will be delayed.

The richness of Spirit is such that it has blessings one-thousandfold that are yours by divine right. You do not need to envy or covet what others may have. Your blessings are unique. They are fitted just for you. They are custom-made.

The needs of each of us are different, depending upon our makeup. It is our right to desire health, success and wholeness. It is our right to love and be loved, and to expect that the dearest desire of our heart will be fulfilled.

Say to yourself right now:

I know Infinite Intelligence takes good pleasure in giving me the Kingdom. I open myself to the right consciousness to receive. I know the riches of life come to me by way of my own consciousness. I let my consciousness unfold today according to the divine plan for me. I determine the desire of my heart and implant it in the subconscious to be acted upon. I keep steady until my desire manifests.

Letting Our Light Shine

Since life is always being born anew, we should look for new experiences to constantly unfold before us. When we do this we open ourselves to new avenues of expression. We experience levels of our being that we had not contacted before.

We need to recognize that we are spiritual entities in physical form, but as spiritual entities we are not limited to this form. It gives us a means of expressing on this plane of existence. We have a mind that is infinite and a spirit that is omniscient, omnipresent and omniactive.

We need to look beyond the form and recognize that we are formless spiritual beings and that on this plane of expression we are constantly elevating ourselves into new dimensions—not only of awareness, but of growth. Internal growth is different from outer growth. Outer growth takes up space and time, but inner growth does not need space or time.

When we close our minds and our hearts and shut off the connection with our inner being, we cease to progress. We grope in darkness. We become confused. If we insist on narrowing our scope of life, we will not experience the broad, powerful stream of cosmic Power filled with intelligence and love that is available to all. We have yet to touch the real depth of our being. So far, most of us have not scratched through the veneer.

The life you are experiencing today may not consist of more than a blink of the eye when compared to the eternality of your soul or to the Infinite, yet many people seem to think that everything is measured in this one measurable lifespan. Oh, indeed, not! We are living now and we will continue to live, and our awareness of this makes a big difference. It makes the difference between really living and merely existing.

Living calls for you to bring forth and use every part of your innermost being. You need to use every resource of your mind, which is part of the infinite Mind. See all Life as a progressive action. Know that you were created to advance. You were created to contribute to this life in your own unique way. You are here to blaze a new trail of expression. Most importantly, as an infinite being, your most valuable acquisition is spiritual understanding. In the final analysis, the only possessions which will be with you always are those of mind and spirit.

Give no small consideration to the direction of consciousness in which you are growing and advancing.

Of course, you can put your slippers on, sit in a rocker, and look out the window and say, "Life is passing me by." You can deliberately take yourself out of the activity of living keenly, or you can be a part of it. You have a choice.

You must let your light shine and reflect the beautiful Spirit that you are.

To know who you really are will not make you egotistical, but it will let you know that you have a place to fill and that you are important to Life. You have an identity and a purpose in Life, and in a larger sense you are the Life that is happening all about you. You can never be a displaced person or be out of place, for there is always a role for you to fill, a job for you to do. You are at home wherever you are.

Think today:

I am always in the right place, doing the right thing, at the
right time. I always learn and grow through every experi-
ence. Good is what I expect, and good, alone, I accept.

In the Science of Mind, we do not base our teachings on dogma or creed, but on the Truth as we know it. We seek to follow the Spirit within us. This does away with rules and regulations, with dogmas and creeds, with ought's and should's. Jesus told us that the Truth would set us free, but he also told us to go forth and do as he did, that is, live in the Spirit.

When we live in the Spirit, we do not look back as Lot's wife did, nor do we lug our former burdens around with us. We follow new direction. "When you put your hand on the plow," you will remember Jesus saying, "do not look back." When you look back, progress is almost nil, and you plow a crooked furrow.

Say to yourself today:

I am a Spirit-directed individual. I am guided and directed by

Sunshine in my soul.

Shine through me

Love can build a

bridge.

Tues
4:30

Address: _____ zip: _____

CVV2 code on back: _____ for MC/Visa **or** for American Express: _____

4 digits printed above the last 4 numbers of your credit card: _____

For **automatic** charges to your credit card, fill out below:

Gift/Donation $ _____ Frequency: once, weekly, monthly

Annual Per Capita $ _____ ($35.00 each member)

For security, please put in envelope and place in offering plate.

Thank You for Your Support -

the Power within me. I am an avenue of expression through which Life can flow in new and different ways. I am a today person. I do not look to tomorrow with fear and apprehension. I know when tomorrow comes it will bring with it its own special wealth of living and being. So I live today, fully, with the expectation of all good.

Now that you have made the decision to live from the Spirit and be a today person, living in the *now*, avenues of new expression will open before you and you will behold and reflect the glory of Infinite Good in your everyday world.

Lift Your Consciousness

Come alive this day. Come alive with a new spirit. Come alive with a new talent. Come alive with new ideas. Stop brooding about what you don't like and start breeding what you do like. Get out of the corner you have selected. Come out of the corner of being melancholy. Come out of that corner right into the center of life itself. Today know that you are not only expressing, but you are experiencing your true spiritual essence of being. You are experiencing the wholeness and perfection of the infinite Power. You are experiencing and expressing the oneness of Life. Feel your infinite individuality and know, "I am an individual; I am not a copycat; I'm an individual and I come out of the corner of darkness right into the center of life, and in this center of life I express my uniqueness. The individuality of my being is expressing with grace and ease through me."

Add to your life today. Stop subtracting. Add. Add the good. Add the pleasantness. Add the peace. Add. Many of us look at each day and we are subtracting. We take away from this and we take from that. Add to your life.

Let's feel and know today that we're not going to add more

problems, more burdens, more difficulties, or more worry. Let's begin to really feel that we're going to come into the conscious awareness that life is an addition of everything that is joyous, constructive, creative, and productive. Let's leave the plane of negativity and get into a new plane of positive expression. Let's lift our sights. Let's lift our heights. Let's lift our conscious awareness. Let's lift our focus right now.

Climb into a feeling of being alive all over, alive from within, experiencing an aliveness in all that you do. Acknowledge aliveness all around you. Be lifted up into new dimensions of consciousness. You know that if you climb the peak of the mountain, you can see new whole vistas before you. You can see everything.

Climb out of the valley of depression, out of the valley of neglect, out of the valley of fear, out of the valley of the past into that new consciousness where everything is being added. Good is being added. Happiness is being added.

There is a statement in the Old Testament: "Be fruitful and multiply." Every business contact that you make today is not in vain. It shall be fruitful and multiply. Every good thought you think today shall be fruitful and multiply. Every letter you send out shall be fruitful and multiply.

Know with me and say:

Today everything that is creative and constructive in my life shall be fruitful and multiply. I'm alive and I'm alive all over. My mind is alive. My body is alive. My emotions are alive with beautiful feeling. I'm alive and I'm alive all over.

Enter into a renewing process in every part of your being. Think clearly. Feel deeply. Act with a wonderful feeling of aliveness in all that you do. Enter into a deeper awareness of your truth, a greater realization of your divinity. Today, have the courage and the conviction of heart and mind to make a complete turnabout and say: "The real me is now giving birth to a *new* identity." Have the courage to surge ahead with enthusiasm and conviction. Today, let yourself become so in tune with the Infinite that you sense a beautiful rapport with all the beauty and all of the love of life itself. Don't let life pass you by, but get into a beautiful consciousness that "I am one with all life and I am one with the Infinite." When you feel alive, then this aliveness is part of the pulsation of your being. It becomes a tingling feeling, an exciting feeling. A zest begins to move in. You can't sit still when you feel alive. When you really feel alive inside and outside, there is a joy that wells up within you.

Plant a seed of a new consciousness today, the seed of richer expectations and loftier vision that you are moving toward today with the realization that you are one with the Divine Originator. Lift your head up high, throw your shoulders back, look straight ahead with conviction and claim your new lease on life. Feel the aliveness of the energy of love, the dynamic presence of Spirit in you that is expressing by means of you. Be glad you're alive this day.

Chapter Three

~~~

Pain
as Healer

Whatever is to give light must endure burning.

—Victor Frankl

～～～

The moment in which we reach the last depth of our lives is the moment in which we can experience the joy that has eternity within it, the hope that cannot be destroyed, and the truth on which life and death are built. For in the depth is truth; and in the depth is hope; and in the depth is joy.

—Paul Tillich

From time to time we all need to examine our lives, clear out the mental debris and set our thinking in order. Until we do this, our mind is like a beautiful garden that has become so overgrown with weeds that its beauty cannot shine through.

Each spring the roses put out new shoots and leaves before they give us the flowers, but we all know that the gardener, if he wants beautiful roses, cannot let the shoots go out in all directions at random. There is a time when he must prune them for the next blooming. The pruning gives strength and new direction.

To depict the clearing of the consciousness in another way, often we use our minds like crypts or cemeteries. They are burdened with many coffins, urns filled with ashes from the past that should be discarded. They are ashes of doubts, fears, uncertainty and all those negative memories we let intrude upon our lives.

How can we go about changing this condition in ourselves? We must work with consciousness. Changes always begin in consciousness. Suppose you look around you and everything is dark, everything is pitch-black. There seems to be no hope whatsoever. See yourself as a light in the midst of apparent darkness. Jesus said, "I have come that you might have life and have it more abundantly." Life is light and if you can recognize this, you can shine in the darkness about you. Say to yourself right now, "I am the light of my world. I let my light shine. I have the light of understanding, the light of awareness, the light which helps me to accomplish in all my ways. I let my light shine."

Whatever you know about yourself, you are. If all you know about yourself is your weakness, then that is what you must be—not in Reality, but in expression. If you know only your anxieties, then that is what you are—a bundle of nerves. Each individual becomes a manifest expression of his or her self-concept. If you know your strength, if you know your ability and your potential, then that is what you express. You cannot express anything that you do not conceive yourself to be.

It is what you really know in consciousness that counts. If you know you are a light, you can shine in the darkness that threatens to hem you in. If you know and declare yourself to be the light, you will not have to grope in the dark.

The light does not fight the darkness at all. When the light moves in, the darkness moves out. If you struggle and fight the darkness, you will continue to bump into everything about you; but if you simply turn on the light, you can avoid bumping into problems and frustrations.

The light shows you the way to move into new experiences that are far more gratifying than the old ones. Where does this light shine? In your own consciousness. It is the spiritual illumination which ignites the fires of inspiration that move you to commit to your highest dreams and aspirations.

You are always experiencing. Every experience may not be to your liking, but nevertheless you are always moving into new experiences. There is no reason why you should not have experiences which are pleasing. Be aware that by your own thoughts and your own feelings, you create your own experiences.

As long as you accept facts, figures, opinions, and appearances as the Truth, you will never experience the great accomplishments and fulfilling relationships possible for you. Reality, despite what facts, figures, and opinions say, is the ultimate cause. It is the absolute Truth back of all things and events. Your life does not need to include deeply distressing times. It should be fundamentally one joyous experience after another.

Whenever problems arise, you can think creatively and constructively concerning them, or you can let the problems take over. There is an old Chinese proverb which says, "So you have fallen on the ground and you are lying there. How long will you lie there?"

Many of us have fallen down, but must we remain there? We can choose to bounce back, because there is a Power within us which enables us to do so. It is our reaction to those things that happen to us in life that causes us to experience misery or happiness, success or failure, health or illness.

Some people can face a difficulty and come out of that difficulty stronger, greater, wiser and renewed in many ways. Others will face the same difficulty and be defeated by it. It is not the condition. It is our reaction to the condition which creates health or illness. It is our response which causes us to create success or failure in our lives. No condition of itself has the power to shape our destiny, but how we use the situation, how we think about it, and what we feel about it is the key.

today:

*…ot the problems in my life that matter. It is my
…se to them. Any problem is a secondary thing. I can
… tear me to pieces or I can let it bind me more closely
to the Power that is within me. I can let it negate my living
or I can let it stimulate me to greater expression.*

Our emotions can join forces with the imagination in tearing us to pieces when we are in a difficult situation. But when we unite intelligence with the imagination, we become stronger and create a way out of the difficulty. We become stronger rather than weaker. Remember that nothing in your life has power over you that you do not give it. You can let your emotions govern you, or you can direct your emotions. The Infinite gave you the power of choice and a will.

Say to yourself right now:

*I have the power of choice and I use this power to steer
myself in the right direction. I steer in the direction of my
desire. I direct my life. I meet any problems which present
themselves with the calm knowing that if I see and respond
in the right manner, I will become stronger and wiser. I
choose the path of personal responsibility and power.*

Thoughts are occurring in our minds at all times. They exist, but they need direction. Thought has power. Thought is creative. Thought is energy in action, but thought without direction can cause as much harm as good.

Recognize that you have the ability to think. You have emotions. You have the power of imaging, and you also have the power to direct what comes into your consciousness.

True Repentance

The life of Saul, who became Paul after his conversion, is one that can have meaning for all of us. In his early years Paul was anything but kind and considerate of his fellowmen. He was cruel, mean and selfish. He was narrow-minded. After his vision on the way to Damascus, however, his entire life changed completely. The realization he had was so great that he was temporarily blinded to the physical world. He could no longer see things as he had seen them before.

Now, Paul had a multitude of things for which he had to repent. Did his repentance consist of weeping, donning sackcloth and sitting among the ashes? Did he moan and groan and whip himself for his past mistakes? No. He said that what he had done before he had done in ignorance and now that he knew better, he would do better. This he did. Forgetting the things of the past he pressed forward to his mark of high calling.

This is true repentance. True repentance is not indulging in self-pity, weeping about a mistake or beating ourselves over the head with it. That only emphasizes it. True repentance means being converted, that is, turning in a new direction and not repeating the mistake.

Religion throughout the years has attached many unhealthy connotations to the words "repentance" and "conversion." Let's simplify them today and put them in their proper perspective, which is as simple as realizing that we need to turn ourselves in a new direction. To convert means to "turn about." The dictionary gives the following as synonyms: alter, change, interchange, transform, transmute, transpose.

When we repent for something we have done, we atone for it— that is, we make up for it by not doing it again and by doing the right thing instead. Paul's repentance meant a changed life.

It meant getting out of the old rut and into a new and vital way of living. In the light of the new understanding, he did not let the old ignorance have any power over him.

When we break old molds of thought and replace them with new ones, we are repenting. It is not some big and mysterious ritual, though the truth can come to us in many ways. It can come through prayer, study, and meditation, or it can come to us through flashes of intuition and insight. However it comes, it throws a new light on things. We see differently. We feel differently. We act differently.

Illumination is simply seeing more and more of the light that is. Sometimes this light is revealed to us gradually and sometimes it is like a sudden explosion. If we have been stumbling against the furniture in a dark room and light a candle, we see the dim outlines of things. If we turn on the electricity, we see more details; if the same room is flooded with sunlight, everything is still more distinct and clear.

In the same way, the more illumination we derive from spiritual understanding, the more clearly we know the direction our lives should take, and the less we stumble over the things we bumped into in our days of darkness or ignorance. Now that we see them for what they are, they do not have to bother us any more. We can let them be and go on to greater expressions of life.

Begin to break old molds of thought by replacing them with new ones. Do not try to break your husband's or wife's mold. Do not try to break your boss's mold, or that of your children or friends. Look only to your own thoughts.

Your happiness and progress are not dependent upon someone else. You are the cause of your life and you are the effect of your life. You are the cause of your own success and you are the cause of your own failure. You cannot escape this truth, but if you see a new light (that is, if you come to a greater understanding), you can change the cause and in so doing change the effect.

Your mind operates on two different levels. It operates on a conscious or objective level and it operates on a subjective level. What you put into the subjective field of mind with the conscious side of mind comes to pass, for the subjective side of mind acts on the direction of your conscious mind. This makes you a law unto yourself. You select that which you experience, though you are not always aware of your selections.

Do you get up in the morning and select joy, prosperity, happiness and health, or do you select all the gloomy things? You are the selector. You select and your subconscious mind acts to bring into your experience that which you have selected. Many things may appear to just walk into your life without your selecting them, but they have to have an entrance. You had to leave the door open with your thoughts, emotions, and attitudes; otherwise, those things could not walk in.

Begin now to select intelligently. Begin to replace the things you do not want with the things you do want. Remember that you are a spiritual being and your mind is infinite.

If you do not like where you live, if the world seems against you, if people appear unfriendly and ill health plagues you, stop looking at appearances. Begin to implant in your subconscious that which is the truth. The world is not against you. People are basically friendly. Health is your natural state of being. Appreciate where you are and then you can move to where you want to be.

Say to yourself right now:

I am the selector and creator of my life. I build my life on Truth. As I receive new understanding, my past becomes a shadow. I walk in the light and leave the shadow behind.

51

Let us remember that the more spiritual truth we understand, the more adept we can become in using it. We begin to expand in consciousness. We learn that consciousness is the source of all the beautiful and foundational qualities upon which to build our lives. We find good there. We find love there. We find joy there. We find our own true beingness there.

We learn that beauty is not affected by ugliness. Sorrow does not affect the harmony of the universe. We can heal ourselves by knowing the Truth. We can repent by seeing the light of the infinite Creator and recognizing it as the governing power in our lives.

Bounce Back

If you have a slump in your finances, that is all it is—a slump. Beyond the appearance is your perpetual good. You can get right back into business and get going again. The same is true if you are ill or if your relationships are not going smoothly. Wholeness underlies the appearance of illness; harmony underlies the appearance of disrupted relationships.

There is always something to learn through every experience you have, but that does not mean you have to remain in the experience indefinitely. Look upon all problems as temporary and upon all good as that perpetual nourishment which you constantly obtain from Spirit.

The moment you elevate to a new, richer state of consciousness, the appearances in your world will change. Get the beautiful feeling that your good is uninterrupted. You do not have to be concerned about getting what someone else has and I do not have to be concerned about getting what you have. Your good can never be taken away from you. Your good can never be disturbed unless, by your own state of mind, you believe that it can.

We often speak of life as a race and we say that everyone should get in there with the expectation of winning. This is true, but you are not competing with others. You are only endeavoring to better yourself. You are only trying to outdo your own former performances. In this race, we sometimes grow discouraged. We feel it is impossible to go on. Then something happens. We get what in running is called a second wind. We get new energy and strength. We get new hope and courage. What we often fail to realize is that this energy, strength, courage and new vision are always at hand, always awaiting our recognition and acceptance. No matter, then, where you find yourself, think of this second wind and go for your second chance. Your marriage may be in shreds, your relationships at the office may be paper-thin, and your social life may be practically null and void, but if you capture the expectation of a second chance, you will bounce right back and make it.

The winning consciousness is already within you. Life has a bounce, a livingness, but often we hold the bounce down. We look at everything with a negative attitude. Often we are fatalistic: life has just dealt us the wrong cards and all we can do is play them. We never imagine that the deck can be reshuffled and dealt again.

You and I live in the age of mind and we are closer and closer to being able to express more and more of the Spirit within us. We can not afford to be governed strictly by our emotions. We must be governed by our thinking and our thinking must be governed by the infinite Spirit within us. Each individual must become his or her own master. Each individual must take the responsibility for that which he or she creates in life. To follow other people meekly and echo their thoughts does not release you from living your own life. It only prolongs your servitude, which can be terminated any time you determine to take charge of your life.

Many of us, when we first assume full responsibility for ourselves, feel lost and alone. We are as unsteady in our consciousness as an infant is when first learning to walk. But there is Something that makes the toddler get up and try and try again, until finally the task is mastered. The same is true with us. If we determine to live our own life from the center out, that Something will supply us with all the assurance we need.

Remember that thinking and feeling must go hand in hand. They complement one another. In order for you to move ahead toward the goal, your feelings and your thoughts must agree. When they do, you have a strong partnership that will carry you forward to the fulfillment of your desire.

No matter what you affirm, until you have a feeling supporting your affirmation, nothing will happen. When words and feelings are in opposition, it is like a stalemate in a chess game. This is why feeling plays a critical role as the empowering factor that makes your dreams come true.

In spite of what you are experiencing, can you feel that within you are health, happiness, joy, and the power to live a fulfilling life?

Every one of us is a master. What are we masters of? Our own consciousness. Our own thoughts. Our own feelings. Our own words. We master the principles of life and the laws by which it works. We will to be willing to accept our good and not force it. We get our personality out of the way and let the divine circuits take over.

Do not confuse emotion or emotionalism with deep feeling. You can feel deeply without being what is termed an emotional person. Feeling is the acquiescence deep within you to what the mind tells you Life is all about. You sense the Truth by feeling it. Mental acceptance is not enough. There must be an acceptance with your whole being.

Say to yourself right now:

No appearances can keep me down. My faith in the Infinite gives me bounce and comeback. I take my second wind and put more livingness than ever into my life.

Know today that no circumstance can hold you down permanently without your consent. You can discover and uncover the real treasures of consciousness within you. Instead of plodding along in a lethargic manner, get the idea that you are digging for the hidden treasures within yourself, and that each one will be a wonderful surprise, greater than any good you have experienced before.

You Are the Only One

You are the only one who can make you laugh and you are the only one who can make you cry. No one else can make you laugh and no one else can make you cry. No one else can give you anything that your own consciousness will not accept.

You are the only person you can improve upon. You are the only person you can ever change. You cannot change Aunt Sophie, Uncle Harry, the three children, the neighbor across the street, or anyone else. You can only change you. This should give you a great sense of freedom.

Many people think the Science of Mind is a very self-centered approach to life because it puts the attention on me, myself, and I. It is self-centered only because it deals with the center. It is centered on the inner you. It is centered on that point within yourself from which all your knowledge, your life and your guidance flow, and until you know your real self and live your real self, you cannot know and love others. In this manner only is the Science of Mind self-centered. It is not the little self we are interested in, but the big Self, that spark of divinity which has been implanted within each and every one of us.

If I cannot accept myself, I cannot accept you. If I cannot be kind to myself, I cannot be kind to you. If I cannot be joyous within myself, I cannot give joy to you.

Look into yourself then and behold the beautiful you. Look within yourself and find the creative you. Look within yourself and find the loving you. Look within yourself and find the kind you. Look within yourself and find your true nature and then let it come forth.

Jesus did not heal all the people who thronged around him and asked to be healed. Why? Because many of them could not accept the healing within their own consciousness. It is important that you accept yourself, that you know that the stuff within you is good, that the Life within you is good.

There is no such thing as a person being lost or a person being bad. We are all born basically good. It is the nature of the universe to be joyous. It is the nature of the universe to be peaceful. It is your nature to be both peaceful and joyous. If you are not so, begin to reveal your real self. As you do this, you will know that you are a part of the whole. You will know that the center of the Infinite finds its center in you. You will have a deep sense of belonging and this feeling of belonging is the greatest security you can ever know.

Do not look at the universe as a big circle filled with many things. If you do this, you separate yourself. It becomes the observed and you become the observer. Instead, get the feeling that you are centered in the universe. You are not on the outside looking in. You are a part of the whole thing. Think: "Here I am and here is my world all around me. I belong, because a part of everything is within me and I am within a part of everything."

This feeling of belonging takes the craving and gnawing feeling of insecurity away. You no longer feel isolated. You no longer feel separate. You have a feeling of oneness. You sense that the universe cannot be divided against itself. There is no person who can take your place. There is no one who can express exactly like you. Each belongs to life as an essential part of the whole and yet each is free to choose his or her expression. You are free to claim your place in life. Until you do, you will never really experience it.

Many times in a marriage one partner has already quit long before a divorce takes place in the courts. Things are lost in mind long before they are lost objectively. The things that happen to us must happen first in consciousness. They have to be accepted in consciousness first.

You hear people say, "This cannot happen to me," and it does not happen to them if they have fully accepted the statement in consciousness. Whatever they were talking about bypasses them. It goes right around them. You can't be fired from a job unless you fire yourself first in mind. Remember, though, that you accept many things in your mind that you do not say anything about, and this unuttered acceptance makes them possible.

If you hear someone say, "I never thought I would pull through that," you can be sure he is a liar. I do not mean he is lying deliberately, but if deep within him he did not believe that he would pull through, he wouldn't. We demonstrate what we feel. We demonstrate what we believe. We demonstrate what we accept in consciousness.

Be sure of what you are seeking. Do not be like the woman

who prayed for a husband, got him and then prayed that he be taken away. Really know what you want. As soon as you get the consciousness, all the manifestations will appear in your experience.

Say to yourself right now:

The key to freedom, peace, joy and plenty lies within me. What I accept in consciousness manifests in my life. I accept oneness and wholeness with the universe.

You are free today to live your own life, to accept what is right for you and to reject what is wrong for you. Take command of your own life today and let others have the same freedom.

Forgiveness Heals

We must learn to forgive others. We must learn to forgive situations and conditions, but, most of all, we must learn to forgive ourselves. A lack of forgiveness builds up tremendous pressures within ourselves.

If you want to experience better health, sit down and say, "What do I have to forgive? What needs forgiveness in my life?" On the surface you may not be aware of anything that you need to forgive, but if you will sit quietly and think about it, you will become aware of a little grudge here and a little misunderstanding there and a little disagreement somewhere else. You will find that you have not washed them completely out of your system, that like the little grain of sand in the oyster shell, they are still irritating you just a little. Most of all, ask yourself in what ways you have not forgiven yourself. Maybe you can forgive others, but you continue to blame yourself in many areas. Forgive yourself of your mistakes, seeming shortcomings, and apparent inadequacies, and start with a fresh mental attitude.

To forgive means to gain a new sense of peace. To forgive means to replace the old with something new. To forgive means to give up all inharmony. To forgive means to forget that someone has hurt you, or been unkind or inconsiderate. Forgiving and forgetting go hand in hand and you cannot accomplish the forgiveness as long as you are not willing to forget.

Perhaps you say to yourself, "I don't have anything to forgive. I am not holding anything against anyone." This may be true, but if you have any inharmony in your body, if you have any consciousness of unrest, or if things just do not have the zest for you that they should, it pays to sit down and think: "Why do I feel the way I feel? Could it be caused from a lack of forgiveness?" Ask your subconscious mind: "What needs forgiveness in my consciousness? What needs to be forgiven? What has happened in my life up to the present day that needs to be healed? What is it that I have not been able to release? What has happened to me, even though I may have forgotten what it was, that makes me feel bitter?"

Forgiveness is a giving up of one thing so another better thing can come into your life. It is a very freeing process. It leaves you with a clean mental and emotional slate to start fresh and new.

Say to yourself;

Everything that has offended me, I now forgive. I release everything in my consciousness, past or present, which I have been unable to forgive. Whatever it is and whether I am consciously aware of it or not, I release it. I let it go. I start with a fresh, clear consciousness.

It may be something that happened at work. It may be something that happened when you were a child. It might have been something in a first marriage. It may be something that a husband or wife has done to a child, or a neighbor, or something that you have done to yourself. Whatever it might be, great progress will take place when you sit down and say, "Whatever needs forgiveness in my consciousness, I forgive. I drag no burdens of unforgiveness around with me. I travel light and free. I need all of myself clear and unburdened to put into the present living of my life. I free my consciousness of any weights of unforgiveness which have held me back."

The body does not make itself ill. Our affairs do not go awry of their own accord. Our happiness is not manufactured from the outside. That which goes forth from us is that which returns to us in many subtle ways—ways so subtle that we do not always recognize their origin—yet we work diligently to correct things from the outside before looking within to our own consciousness.

Say to yourself:

I forgive everything. I forgive everyone who has ever come into my life that I may hold a subconscious grudge against, a subconscious irritation against, a subconscious ill feeling against.

One little grudge, one little irritation, one little hurt feeling may not impede your progress, but a gradual buildup will. I cannot take the whole telephone book and tear it in half, but if I took a page at a time, I could eventually have the book torn in half. The same is true with all the little things that we harbor in our consciousness. They build up until they accomplish just what we do not want to experience in our lives.

This is why it is important at times to ask yourself, "How forgiving and how understanding am I? How loving am I?" Individuals who are so sensitive that they carry their feelings on their sleeves are not individuals who are loving. Our sensitivity should be of a different nature. We should be sensitive to things of the Spirit and not to the hurts we collect. Say to yourself often,

"I am free from whatever has brought this irritating thought to me. I am free of it. I free everyone and am thereby free myself. I hold nothing against anyone."

Work with your own consciousness. You are not responsible for the consciousness or the acts of another. No matter how justified you may feel to hold grudges or be unforgiving, there is no justification strong enough for you to let unforgiveness affect your life adversely.

Hold on to no one. Hold on to nothing. Hold nothing against anyone, in any way, shape or form. This does not mean that you have to get cozy with all people. No, the important thing is that you do not hold anything against them in your consciousness. When we hold anything against anyone in our consciousness, then we are holding ourselves back, because it is our own mind which is filled with the pollution of anger, blame and negation.

True forgiveness is the greatest healing power that ever existed. Quickly you will say, "I thought love was the greatest healing power in the universe." We cannot forgive without loving. The letting go and the loving follow hand in hand. If you love, you are not holding grudges. If you forgive, you love, and you are not holding grudges. I am not speaking of love and forgiveness as big emotional upheavals, but as deep understanding and a willingness to go along with life. With this understanding comes the realization that our hurts and grudges are petty compared to what love and forgiveness can do.

Don't forgive to make someone else feel better. Do it to right your own life—to free your own consciousness.

Any dis-ease will bear inspection in terms of the need to forgive. There is nothing humiliating in forgiving and forgetting, yet some people feel that they lose face if they forgive. They do not lose anything except those things which have been detrimental, those things which have been weighing them down, those things which have been impeding their progress.

Healing in any area of your life cannot help but take place when you become truly forgiving and truly loving, so if everything is not one hundred percent perfect in your life today—try forgiving. You will like the results.

Dealing with Depression

"Should I?" "Shouldn't I?" "Maybe so." "Maybe no." "Is this best?" "Is this better?" This fighting with ourselves back and forth causes exhaustion and depression. You will hear indecisive people say, "I feel totally exhausted. I am totally depleted." Is it any wonder?

How can we get out of these moody cycles of depression, exhaustion, and physical illness? I believe we can do it by realizing that the consciousness within us is capable of supporting us in our decision-making. It can set the energy flowing again. We can depend on the life within us to keep circulating through us. Our part is to keep on center and "decide to decide."

When you feel exhausted, look within yourself and determine if you are dragging excess baggage about with you because you hesitate to make clear-cut decisions about your life. Of course, some decisions are more important than others, but through inner guidance we can make even the most important ones without taking an excessive amount of time to do so. Objectively we could never finish weighing the pros and cons, but subjectively we can know what is the better course to take.

Some people say, "I don't feel good in cloudy weather." When they do that, what they are really saying is, "Weather, you have control over me. You have power over me. Sun, you are the one that makes me happy. Clouds, you have power over me. You make me sad."

If we let the weather or anything else on the outside determine our moods and our feelings and our reactions, we are giving power to something outside of ourselves.

We need to know that our energy is inexhaustible, that no one and nothing can take our energy from us. When we give power to things outside ourselves, we are off-center, so the first and the most important decision to make is to get back on center and look at the world from that perspective.

For example, as long as we pay our electric bills, plug in an appliance and turn on the switch, we have electricity flowing. The moment we turn off the switch and unplug the cord from the socket, the electricity stops flowing. But the electrical potential is still there, though we are not meeting the conditions required for the use of it. The same is true when we maintain our connection with the center of our being. As long as we do not turn off the switch, we have the current of life flowing through us freely, but if we let anything interfere with our contact, then we begin to experience lack in some form, though the power of Life has not been diminished.

Believe me, no matter what your lack is today, the current is still available. Make your connection. Tune in. When you do so, this Power will flow through you. If you need wisdom to make certain decisions, it will come to you. You will simply know, and you will act with confidence.

Perhaps you feel that the pendulum has swung so far in one direction that there is no hope. But remember a pendulum is free to move back and forth. It is not fixed in one spot. Decide, then, that you will swing the pendulum to the other extreme and know the fullness of joy, the richness of life, and the power to act.

Many of your problems are just old habit patterns to which

you are responding. The feeling of emptiness can become a habit, as can depression, as can giving power to the outer world, and as can indecision. When you swing the pendulum in the other direction, you will no longer respond in these old ways. You will respond with newness to the fullness of Life and creativity within you.

Within you is the power to be yourself. Jesus dared to live his own life, to be himself. He kept contact with his Source. He did not try to copy anyone else. He was not here to imitate. He was here to take leadership in life. He was showing by example that each of us is unique and endowed with the creative power of Life to express our uniqueness—as long as we keep a conscious contact with our Source intact.

Why not decide to tackle something new today? By so doing, you can enlarge your consciousness. You can move into a whole new aspect of life. You can swing the pendulum in the other direction. If I told you to take a pen and paper and write down a hundred failures in your life, you would probably get busy without comment, but if I told you to write a hundred successes, you would groan and say: "A hundred! Who has had a hundred successes?"

See! We are prone to talk about our problems, to remember the failures, the heartaches, the setbacks. We are geared in this direction. That is why we must swing the pendulum to the other extreme. Life is filled with successes but we have to recognize them. We have to decide to talk and think success instead of problems and failures.

Decide today to find the center of your being and to express from this center. Decide to be your own unique self. Decide to tackle something new. Decide to emphasize your successes, even the smallest and simplest.

It is seeing the little successes instead of mistakes or

failures that will help you swing your reactions to success instead of failure. If you are a good cook, that is a success. If you are a good wife and mother, chalk these up in your favor. If you sew a fine seam, if you grow or arrange beautiful flowers, if you are a good father, if you are friendly with people, if you are good at your job, chalk these up in your favor. You do not have to be President or win the Pulitzer Prize to be a success. The greatest success of all is to let Life fill you with itself, so you can rejoice and express what you really are.

Say to yourself today:

I am a decisive individual. I make decisions easily. I turn within, listen and obey the instruction of the Divine in me. I know without analyzing and arguing with myself what is right for me. I am a success in life, because I keep the contact with my Source intact. I always work from the center out. Every day presents me with a multitude of choices and they are not difficult to make, because I am constantly exercising my spiritual muscles and am ready for any task that confronts me.

As you make the decision today to stand on your own feet, you will no longer be a leaner. You will not have to be propped up by outer conditions, people, or things. You will drop all your invisible crutches. You will decide to be yourself and let others be themselves, and you will realize what a beautiful, wonderful world you live in and how wonderful you yourself are.

Chapter Four

~~~

Be Excited
About Life

Every great and commanding moment in the annals of the world is the triumph of enthusiasm.

—Ralph Waldo Emerson

~~~

Enthusiasm is the yeast that makes your hopes rise to the stars.

—Henry Ford

~~~

We must blow on the coals of the heart.

—Archibald MacLeish

*W*e are only true to ourselves when we acknowledge that Spirit within us is infinite, that life is ongoing, and that the soul is indestructible. We are only true to ourselves when we know that we have a great contribution to make to life and that life created us to succeed, to advance in consciousness and to express in our time/space world with abandonment to the divine will within us.

We are not true to ourselves when we let the world crowd in upon us and pressure and weigh us down with its contrary appearances. If the Spirit within is pushing forth through us, no pressure on the outside can withstand it. It knows no time, space, nor obstacle. It proceeds joyously and lovingly on its way, "creating worlds before it and leaving worlds behind it."

This does not mean that we will not meet with all varieties of experience, nor does it mean that we will never know pain or sorrow. It does mean that in the midst of every appearance to the contrary, we will know that the living Spirit is always present, empowering us to move out of the condition, the pain, into well-being and wholeness once more.

Life is everywhere present, even in the darkest darkness. When we are surrounded by darkness, whether it be emotional, mental, or physical, we can either succumb hopelessly to it or we can kindle that spark of life that is in the midst of it and start a blaze that will light our way out of it.

We may live under the shadow of darkness. We may live in a world where chaos is apparent. We may find great areas of opposition. This seems to be the case every time we turn on the television and hear the news, or read a paper or a magazine, but all of this negation cannot stop us if in consciousness we dwell on the Light.

We must prepare to live. There must be a great curiosity within us and an interest that will not give up. We must be aware of the truth, which is that, seen in the light of the divine, everything is all right. "The Infinite rests in Its smiling repose." We are speaking here of the spiritual world, the reality back of the appearance world, the divine spark at the center of all things.

Life is a beautiful and challenging experience. It is up to us whether we see beauty or dwell upon ugliness. It is up to us whether we accept the challenge to grow and unfold more of the potential within us, or choose to look upon every challenge as a barrier that would deliberately thwart us.

In the process of learning and growing, we may fall down many times, but we have the power to bounce back if we will just use it.

Say to yourself today:

Today I will be truly myself. I will so activate the divine spark within me that nothing can defeat me, nothing can keep me frustrated, nothing can loom larger than the power within me to cope with it. I am in reality a spiritual giant. I am expressing the fullness of my glory and beingness. The shadows of the world cannot darken my life, for through the infinite power within me I become the light of my own world.

Yes, within you is a pearl of great price, which makes you a dynamic individual capable of accomplishing whatever you set out to do.

When any dark spot appears in your life, remember the words of the 139th Psalm: "Whither shall I go from thy spirit? Or whither shall I flee from thy presence? If I ascend up into heaven, thou art there: If I make my bed in hell, behold, thou art there. If I take the wings of the morning, and dwell in the uttermost parts of the sea; even there shall thy hand lead me, and thy right hand shall hold me. If I say, surely the darkness shall cover me; even the night shall be light about me. Yea, the darkness hideth not from thee; but the night shineth as the day: the darkness and the light are both alike to thee."

Freedom of Choice

Each person is here on this plane of expression to play out the game of life. Some of us play a winning game and some of us play a losing game. This does not mean that we are governed by fate. It means that each of us creates our own fate at the level of our own understanding. Each of us is where we are because of how we use our freedom of choice. If we would not simply drift through life, we must not allow ourselves to be tossed to and fro as the ocean tosses its debris to and fro until it throws it upon the shore. We do not have to drift or be tossed about like debris.

There is something within us that says "I can." Why don't you say that right now where you are—"I can"—and at this point, the moment you say "I can," something begins to change. The moment you realize "I can," that is followed up with "I will." Why don't you say that silently to yourself right now. "I can and I will." I *will* begin to allow things to happen in my life for the better. I *will* begin to realize the ability within me. I know *I can* change my life for the better and I *will* begin right now!

No matter how terrible conditions may appear, no matter how chaotic the world around us seems to be, life is beautiful and there is nothing wrong with you; there is everything right about you. Stop looking at what is wrong; stop picking on you, stop attacking you; stop pulling yourself apart and start knowing there is nothing wrong with the life that is in you. The life in you is beautiful, wonderful and harmonious.

We cry out, "Why doesn't God change the world? Why doesn't someone change situations and conditions?" But we are co-creators with the Infinite and are responsible for creating our own world. We have a choice today—to live life fully or to live in a limited way. Depending on how we use our freedom of choice, we can make this day heaven or hell.

We are placed here among the riches of the universe. We are given the power to be kings and queens, to rule over our lives, yet we go about on our hands and knees, surrounded by abundance. Many of us are spiritually starved and bankrupt in the midst of plenty.

Getting on the right track is recognizing that in the spiritual kingdom there are no changes necessary. The kingdom of heaven is within you and the kingdom of heaven is already perfect. It is we who must get on the right track and realign ourselves in our own thinking. When we cooperate with Universal Law, we find the reservoir of good open. Yes, it is open. Life does not keep us in bondage; we keep ourselves in bondage.

If we dig a hole and fill it with water, it will only hold a certain amount of water. It will hold water according to its size.

The deeper the hole, the more liquid it will contain. And the same is true in our lives. We can decide to live in a limited way or we can enlarge the container of our belief.

Say to yourself, "Today I enlarge my trust, I enlarge my consciousness, and I discipline myself to move in a constructive direction." When the mind is disciplined, no matter what comes into our lives, it cannot throw us back more than a moment. We have the power to rise up again.

If we want to get the most out of life and the most out of ourselves, then we must train our thinking. We begin by knowing that there is no life apart from Spirit. There is only one Mind and that Mind is perfect. Universal Intelligence is in us and we are using this creative Mind at all times. We know that Spirit in us is always for us and Divine Mind doesn't give us any opposition. If opposition appears, it is humanly created. If there is chaos in our life, we have attracted it or even created it. How wonderful to know that if we have created the undesirable, we can create the opposite. There is a creative power within each and every one of us that works through us. The power for good is within us. Let's begin building ourselves up. Let's begin by supporting ourselves. Let us see ourselves as pure energy, pure light and pure love, attracting our good and repelling that which we do not desire. Let us lift our consciousness, and we will find that life will reward us openly.

Say to yourself right now:

Today in this new vision and in this new consciousness, I give birth to the awareness that Spirit in me makes everything possible and Universal Intelligence expresses through me. I am centered in Spirit and Divine Mind functions perfectly through me.

Look for Clues

Feel today that you are entering into a new excitement of being. See this day as an exciting adventure. Look for the best in life; look for the opportunities. Know that infinite good is at hand right here and right now. If you feel you are entering into that valley of despair, get back up there into the feeling that life is a joyous thing. Say to yourself, "I am living a life of joy. I am living a life of happiness now."

It is not merely saying these words which will help you, but the act of moving away from negation in consciousness and focusing your attention on the dynamic qualities of life. Retrain yourself along more constructive lines of thinking. This retraining will permit what is natural and good for you to express through you, but you must prepare the way. You cannot waver between positive and negative and get a constructive result.

Capture the spirit of adventure. Open your eyes to the opulence of life about you and to the marvelous power that is within you.

Within you this moment is the opportunity to make newness take place in your life. You can get out of the same old routine. Say, "I am. I can. I will. New life is surging through me at this very minute." You are not foolishly blindfolding yourself and saying that adverse situations and circumstances do not exist, but you are realizing that you have emphasized them too much, to the neglect of the constructive factors of life. Now you are shifting the gears; you are retraining your thoughts and feelings in a different direction.

Whatever you entertain in consciousness is what materializes in your outer world. Jesus said, "I go to prepare a place for you...." Your thoughts and your feelings go before you to prepare your experience for you.

Life is forever offering you a beautiful opportunity to reach out and become something bigger and better, to express something more than you are expressing at this moment. You need to let more of the splendor out.

There are clues all around you, if you just become aware of them. Every time you feel blue, that is a clue. Every time you feel sad, that is another clue. Every time you feel worried and fearful, here you have other clues. These clues are saying, "You are restricting and limiting your consciousness. Get into the stream of life and beauty. Uplift your consciousness today."

Today, be aware of all these restrictions and then dissolve them by discontinuing the beliefs that fed them, knowing that every good thing you desire is possible, that there is a beautiful side of life which you can experience. Look about you. Even in the physical world everything is growing and unfolding. Everything is increasing. So should it be in your life.

As everything grows and unfolds, changes take place. Do not resist change. There can be no growth without it. It only becomes painful when we resist and resent it, or when we fear it. Take change in your stride, knowing it is for growth. Release yourself from the past. Be free.

Another clue is feeling sorry for yourself. Stop seeking sympathy. Do you really want people thinking of you in a negative manner? Do you want them to think of how beaten and downtrodden you are? Would you not rather have them say, "What a wonderful contribution you are making to life!" Look for better ways of getting attention.

Do you want to draw more unhappiness to you, or do you want to radiate that which will attract more life and more beauty to you? We do not solve problems by concentrating on them. We do not get rid of worry by wallowing in it. We do not regain our health by thinking only of our illness, nor does happiness come from enumerating all the things that make us unhappy.

Now and then, we all experience highs and lows. We all have moods, and the temperature of these moods goes up and down. If this were not true, we would live on a monotonous level all of the time. Life would be dull and uninteresting. But we have conditioned ourselves to expect repetitions of certain negative moods by letting ourselves indulge in them too often. We can create more pleasurable moods with the same method.

When you look at a seemingly impossible situation and wonder how it can change, stop wondering *how* and decide that you are going to change your thinking about it now. When you take a stand, the situation or trouble will change. The old cannot abide in a new state of consciousness. Don't talk about the problem. Don't think about it. And how do you do this? By focusing your mind on the solution. Look about you. Be aware of the clues in your life that are telling you to go in one direction or another, then take the direction indicated.

If you will look for and follow the clues that come up, you will begin to grow and expand. There will be a new excitement about life that you have not experienced before. Each day will be a miracle of beauty and glory to you.

Say to yourself now:

Thank you, Infinite Intelligence, for the newness that is taking place in my life right at this moment.

The Best Medicine

Everything that exists has a hidden, unseen source and this is true also of our states of mind. A job, our home, or certain people may give us a temporary feeling of happiness or safety but that feeling is easily disrupted by any breeze that blows if there is not within us a genuine sense of spiritual security and oneness with life itself.

Did you ever try to make unhappy individuals happy? You may have amused them temporarily, but you did not convert them to happiness. They must do that for themselves.

Neither people, places, things, nor jobs will not make us happy, but when we are happy within ourselves, our whole world is bright and beautiful.

We read in the Bible, "A merry heart doeth good like a medicine." Doesn't this passage give us some hint as to how we can change our outer world? Medications are given today for practically every ailment under the sun—to quiet the nerves, to calm and steady the heart, to keep the blood circulating, to cleanse the body internally. But these are only temporary measures.

A merry heart would make most medications unnecessary, for it would keep the blood circulating, steady the nerves, regulate the heart and keep us in a normal state of well-being. A merry heart is one that is not caught in monotony. It is also one that is in tune with Spirit. Monotony takes the elasticity out of a youthful mind and makes it old, but a merry heart keeps the mind alert and actively engaged in life.

It does not matter how many people are interested in you. Their interest in you will not make up for your own lack of interest in life. That is why I say no one can make another individual happy. No one can give another individual a new and abiding interest in life. No one can give another happiness. All of these qualities or states of mind and heart come from within us.

Sometimes we become separated from the springs of happiness within us by determining to see something through to the bitter end. We remain in unrewarding jobs, frustrating situations, or incompatible partnerships because at one time we made a wrong choice. Or perhaps we did not make a wrong choice at that time, but a purpose has been served and it is time to grow and move to another level.

Should you become filled with boredom, frustration and tension, stop and assess your choices. Each of us has a saturation point. See if you have reached this point with regard to something in your life. If life is becoming uninteresting, that may mean you are not letting newness come in. You may be clinging to something that should be released.

We become dull from the center of ourselves before this grayness reflects in our world. The world becomes dull in our minds before it looks dull to our eyes.

Ask yourself today: "Am I truly happy? Am I vitally interested in life?" If your answer is no, then ask yourself again: "What is bothering me? What makes me want to walk away from everything?" Find out what is gnawing at you and upsetting your perceptions of the world.

As foreign as the idea may be to you first, whatever is causing your unhappiness is something you are doing to yourself or allowing to be done to you. Life is always challenging you to find interest and newness. Of course, it makes many demands, but you are equipped to handle them. If a carpenter had every power tool in his tool shed and tried to do all of his work with a handsaw and tack hammer, you would think him stupid. Well, you are equipped with every mental power tool conceivable, so get acquainted with them and put them to use. Build a happy outer life with your inner materials and spiritual tools.

Happiness is the result of a direct knowing of yourself, and it is through this knowing that regeneration takes place within you. Do not cover your life with a gray coating, but decide today to polish it with joy and beauty. To have a happy life requires discipline and the assuming of responsibility—not the kind that sees things to the bitter end but the kind that responds to life day by day, fulfilling the demands of that day and releasing the finished day for a new one.

If you live deeply, creatively, responsively today, you can let go of it, for you have fulfilled it—filled it full—and you are ready for something new and interesting. You do not have to get a new job, a new life, or a new home to experience newness. Life is ever changing, and if you are keeping pace with life, you will experience this newness and happiness where you are without jumping from one thing to another.

Say to yourself today:

The wellspring of happiness is within me. I let it bubble forth fresh and new, keeping my life joyful and interesting. Because there is joy within me, I behold joy in the world about me. Because there is interest in me, my outer world is interesting. My consciousness is as bright as the shining sun. There are no gray clouds of consciousness to make my outer world gray. I keep pace with life. I respond to its challenges and responsibilities, gladly fulfilling each day as I live it in joy, peace, and perfect contentment.

Facing Today

Jot down what you want to experience today. Write down the hunches you get and evaluate them. Take a pencil and pad with you during the day to capture good ideas that come your way. Writing something down impresses it on your mind, and doing something about it cuts the impression still deeper.

Contemplating what a wonderful day is before you to be lived will help make the day wonderful. Mental practice—playing the game only in mind, whether it be golf, basketball, bowling or tennis—improves the actual physical act more than if you dedicated many hours exclusively to physical practice.

Start your day in mind first and your day will be brighter and go more smoothly. If you have people problems or situation problems, reposition yourself in consciousness instead of trying to change other people. Do not simply wish for the situation to change or the individual to move away. Establish yourself aright in mind. You must first find peace within yourself to see peace in another person. You must first see divine perfection within yourself to experience the divine perfection of another.

Life is one great creative adventure and as we go forth to face each day, let us be prepared in consciousness. If life appears to beat us back at every turn, if we feel held back or down, let us remember the spiritual power within us and prepare our day before we move into the living of it.

Life is rich and filled with opportunity for you—for everyone—but you must be open and available to this opportunity and move out and express it fully. Your Creator made you happy—made you loving—made you complete. Universal Intelligence made you of the very substance of itself. You are, in potential, everything that the Allness is. There is no reason for withdrawing from facing this day. It is the day the Infinite has made for you; learn to rejoice in it and be glad.

Today is waiting for you to live it. There is no need to fear it or dread it. Welcome it with an open heart and an eager mind. Be prepared in consciousness for the best and the best will meet you each hour of the day.

Chapter Five

~~~

Treasure Search

All men should strive to learn before they die what they are running from, and to, and why.

–James Thurber

~~~

Lay not up for yourselves treasures upon earth, where moth and rust doth corrupt, and where thieves break through and steal: but lay up for yourselves treasures in heaven, where neither moth nor rust doth corrupt, and where thieves do not break through nor steal: for where your treasure is, there will your heart be also.

–Matthew 6:19-21

Υou are always becoming. You are always unfolding, always moving forward. Each day can be for you a glorious experience, a new avenue of expression. If you expect each day to be the same as the one before it, your expectancy can cause you to miss some wonderful opportunities. Each day should hold a new surprise for you, a new delight, a new excitement.

We all have a purpose in life. We have a cause, a reason for living. We should answer these questions for ourselves: Why am I here? Where do I go from here? What is my purpose?

Our reason for being will be found within ourselves. If we allow Spirit to speak, the still, small voice within us will give us the answer. Then we will know our purpose, just as Jesus knew his. He said, "To this end was I born; for this cause came I into the world that I should bear witness unto the truth." Knowing our purpose will orient us in the direction we are to go. When we stay in tune with Spirit, many possibilities and ways of carrying out our purpose will be revealed to us.

We need some broad plans and goals in our lives, but our lives should not be so rigidly planned that there is no room for the unexpected. Our plans should not be so set that we dare not let a single item get out of place. I do not mean we have to be disorganized. There is a difference between being organized and being crystallized, set, and fixed.

When we are organized everything runs in a harmonious manner, but to be crystallized and set is to live by routine. When we live merely by routine, we cannot tolerate the least change in our plans, but when we are in tune with the Spirit, we welcome changes, knowing they can inspire and lift us. If we let Spirit have its way with us, we will never go far afield, but we will experience new dimensions of consciousness that make our days lighter and brighter.

The Infinite is always harmonious and orderly, never set, never rigid. It has infinite latitude in which to express in surprisingly new and different ways. Let us have a feeling of surprise for each new day. Surprises will turn out to be great if we are flexible, if we can move with the tide, if we can adjust to something that we did not expect.

We need to let go of former ways and former things and live in tune with Spirit today. As we maintain our conscious contact with Spirit, letting it move through us in all our actions, we will not have to plan so minutely. Speakers will really speak from inspiration; artists will paint from inspiration; and all will know what it is like to awake to newness each day.

To live by Spirit does not mean that Spirit is going to do for us what we should do for ourselves. A pianist has to train the hands, mind and feelings to work together, but Spirit inspires the music. A writer has to learn the construction of sentences and paragraphs, the meaning of words, syntax and the like, but if he or she is an inspired writer, the inspiration comes from on High. The same is true whatever our purpose, whatever our walk of life. We prepare the instrument to the best of our ability and then let our higher self operate through it.

The teacher of teachers is within you. You do not have to wander around the world to find a great teacher, a prophet, or a guru. However great a teacher may be, you are the one who must ask yourself the most important questions of life and you are the one who must answer them.

If you will become still, answers will come to you. It will be revealed to you that you are an individual expression of the living Spirit. You have allowed your thinking to become so conditioned by the world that you may have forgotten who you are. Instead of letting the world or any external thing dictate to you, you should be dictating to it—directing it, guiding it.

Say to yourself, "Divine Knower within me, reveal to me what I shall do." Many of us are like doubting Thomas; we do not believe anything that we cannot touch or otherwise experience with the senses. We are still working exclusively at the sense-level of consciousness. It might be well to remember that there are higher counterparts of our five physical senses and that when we train ourselves, we experience different levels of consciousness. "In my father's house are many mansions," as Jesus said, many levels of awareness, many dimensions of consciousness, many areas of knowingness.

Think of yourself as this stately mansion with its many rooms. Think of the grandeur and surprise that you may behold as you go from one room, one dimension of consciousness, to another. You can look at yourself in two different ways: as finite and limited, as having to do and get everything the hard way, or as a son or daughter of Infinite Intelligence, living in a stately mansion called life, in which all the grandeur and beauty is there to behold.

Why see your life in terms of a shambles when you have the

choice of seeing it as a mansion? If your life seems a shambles now, remember the promise, "I will restore unto you the years that the locusts have eaten." The prodigal son "came to himself" and restored his life. Say to yourself today:

I have come to myself, my higher inner self. My mind is restored. My health is restored. My strength is restored. My courage is restored. I am brought back to my original state.

The Spirit within you is ever present. The love within you is always right where you are. The possibility for restoration of any kind is always within you, awaiting your acknowledgment of it. Bring everything up to the present. Do not be governed by what has been.

Say to yourself:

Nothing is lost. All has not failed. Life is for me and the power within me can renew all things.

It is, indeed, a marvelous opportunity that you have, that we all have. We have been entrusted with all the qualities of the Infinite, a mind that is limitless, a love that is pure and all encompassing, and a Spirit so clear that nothing and no one can dampen it. The only thing that can come between us and our higher calling is our own state of consciousness and we have the power to remove the barriers, whatever they are, and let Spirit shine through.

See yourself as infinite Mind in operation. See yourself totally inseparable from your Source. Know that it is impossible, absolutely impossible, to be separated from the Source of your being. See yourself as a spiritual being and your body as a form through which you express. See yourself free from conditioned thinking. Free yourself in consciousness and you will free yourself from all physical bondage and from distorted emotional states. Determine that you are going to set yourself free by living the life of Spirit.

Effective Living

Life on every level is filled with a livingness that is so magnificent and broad that we cannot encompass it with our finite ways of thinking. The world about us is beautiful and filled with wonderful things, but it is not in this outer expression of life that we will find our security. The invisible Presence is within us, and it is here we must look.

This Presence, though you cannot physically touch it, can be leaned upon, depended upon. It is a firm foundation, even though it is abstract. Though invisible, it is more real that anything your senses can tell you. It is right where you are—all-knowing, all-powerful, all-present. All life stems from it and exists in it.

To realize this Presence within you will give you a faith that cannot be shaken and make you a channel through which it can express more bountifully. I am not asking you to have a blind faith, but a knowing faith in the one Power, the one Presence. You must feel that you are located in this Power, that you are this Power.

Dare, then, to believe and have a complete reliance on spiritual principle. In this outer world of appearances, there are unnumbered uncertainties and anxieties, if you judge by appearances. What, then, is the value of your faith and your beliefs? None, unless you really accept that there is something within you to lean upon. Say with assurance, "I believe. I trust. I know. I accept the reliability of the ominipresent Power."

That something deep within you thought you into existence. That something is First Cause, Mind, Infinite Intelligence, Divine Love. That something must be the Original Thinker, the Original Substance, the Original Life from which all existence springs. There cannot be an expression of life in which Infinite Intelligence is not fully present.

Say to yourself:

I realize deep within me that a Divine Power leads me. I know this Power directs me. The Presence inspires me. Wherever I am, it is; whatever it is, I am.

We can be filled with intellectual theories, but until they become something real to us, they will not change our lives for the better. We must know beyond a doubt that the whole universe is an outcome of this Great Something. We must know that we are centered in it and that it is centered in us. We must know that when we are experiencing less than good in some way we have gotten off-center in consciousness and we must get back.

When you awaken to the fullness of your being and utilize your potential, then you are expressing your greatness. You need not measure yourself by Einstein or Jesus, or compare your life to that of Albert Schweitzer. You are unique and you must follow your own unique pattern of expression. When Jesus said, "Follow me," he did not mean, "Mimic me." He meant to follow the way he lived, that is, from the center of his being, out. Measure up to the potential with which you have been divinely endowed. That will bring out your greatness.

Beethoven did not try to be Mozart or vice versa. When you try to be someone else or follow the footsteps of someone else, you deny your own greatness. You deny life an opportunity to express in a new and different way through you. See your whole life on a larger scale than before—your home life, your business life, your social life, every aspect of your living. Seek harmony on a greater scale; seek love on a broader scale. Seek creative expression on a larger scale.

Say to yourself, and feel it:

How beautiful it is to know that I am life. I am life and I am living my life to the fullest of my potential. I envision living on a larger scale every day.

Effective living is available to each and every one of us. It is not limited to just a few. But to live effectively requires directive thinking. We must think in a directive manner and not in a whirlpool of emotions.

There are certain things that we do well and certain other things that we do not do as well. We must build upon what we are able to do. We must find the talents and potentials within us and utilize them. If there are things you have no affinity for at this time, let them go. You do not have to do everything that everyone else does. Specialize in your own way. Some have a gift for singing, others for painting, others for writing. Still others are talented in a craft, in business or in a profession.

Ask yourself what you are drawn to and what you can do well, and then do it. All of life is beautiful and whatever talent you choose, you can express it beautifully.

Your purpose for being here is to enlarge your spiritual awareness and to live more effectively each day, which means to live more in accord with the forward-moving processes of life. Say to yourself:

I do not have to do everything, but I do have to do something. I have to do that to which I am drawn, that for which I have a strong affinity, and I have to do it well. Effective living is living from the center out. Today, I begin the beautiful process of enlarging my circle of awareness and deepening my consciousness of truth. I am a magnet through which spiritual power expresses out into my world.

We grow by meeting every challenge. See yourself today as beautiful in every way. See the day as beautiful. See people as beautiful and meet every challenge with confidence, knowing that something good will happen from it.

Blueprints

Know today that within you is a Power and a Presence. There is a treasure house of knowledge within you. There is a treasury of ideas, but only when you come to know these things and rely upon them can you bring them forth.

Dissolve within your mind a belief in shortages. There are no shortages. There are appearances, but there are not shortages. Every appearance of a shortage is an effect. In Mind there are no shortages, because thought is unlimited and universal Substance is everywhere present, waiting to take the form of our thought. Whatever you might need is always right there, at the right time, in the right place. Think great thoughts, abundant thoughts. Add to your thoughts strong feelings and convictions that the universe is always in perfect agreement with your richest aspirations.

When we experience shortages, we are caught up in negativity. We must work to avoid adopting that attitude of mind. If we know we are always provided for, we will know that we never have to go without. When we declare the truth of the abundance of the universe, we should not declare it for ourselves only but for others also.

Everything has a cycle and at the conclusion of this cycle, the Infinite brings forth something new and different. Life is constantly refining itself. Know, then, that when anything draws to a conclusion in your life, something new and beautiful, something more refined and efficient will come along.

Develop a feeling that within you is a treasure. It is within every person, but we all must discover this for ourselves. Great men and women of the past have known about this treasure within and have employed various means of accessing it. We all have this treasure within and the ability to contact and experience its riches.

All right. You have this treasure within. How do you mine it? You do it through the power of the subconscious mind. You must learn to rely more and more upon this power. It has the answer to any and all problems with which you may be faced.

You must be willing to take time to develop the use of your subconscious mind. If you bought a government bond tomorrow, you would not be able to cash it in the next day for its face value. You would have to wait until it matured to realize its full value. The same is true with the use of your mind. It takes time and effort to train yourself to depend upon the subconscious and to trust it to give you the answers.

It is not the subconscious mind which needs time. It is our personal requirement to overcome our resistance to change. After this is accomplished, we come into the right consciousness and the right ability to use it. This is why we can say, "Your good is only a thought away." Your good, in fact, is as close in time and space as it takes you to believe and accept.

True maturity brings you into a greater understanding of life and the way it operates. You mature into an awareness of your inner nature. As you do this, things begin to increase for you. You start with an idea. This idea may be one of health, wealth, right relationships, or creative self-expression. Whatever the idea is, you nurture it and let it drop into the subconscious mind to grow in value and express in your outer life.

When you know that the subconscious mind is the builder within you, you will learn to give it an idea upon which to work and release it to produce the manifestation in its own way. It can build and rebuild your body. It can heal your wounds of whatever nature. It can do the seemingly impossible when it is teamed up with clear and conscious direction. It does not initiate. The conscious mind must do that, but it will take what the conscious mind provides and work it out in detail. The subconscious mind does not question. It simply acts upon what it is given to work with. Your subconscious mind depends upon the plans you lay before it.

Each night for the next week, take ten minutes before going to sleep and promise yourself, "For the next ten minutes, I am going to feed my subconscious mind with the most prosperous, healthful, and constructive ideas that I can think of. This is construction, or building time. I am preparing the plans for the subconscious to work upon." Then proceed to do just that. Let no negative thoughts enter in. Tell them to step aside. Keep bringing yourself back to the constructive side of thinking.

Remember, every time you think, you set up a cause. This cause ultimately becomes the effect, the condition, the thing you experience. Take advantage of the treasure house within you. Let your faith eventuate in the fulfillment of your heart's desire.

Say:

I am the builder of my life. I draw the plans with which my subconscious mind works. I am careful to release to it only those thoughts and feelings which I want to see manifested in my outer life. I am successful in all avenues of my life.

You Are Rich Now

If you want abundance in your life, you must claim it in your consciousness. When you do this you are expressing the law of abundance that is within you and all around you. You are not only realizing that you are a son or a daughter of an infinite Intelligence, but you are also recognizing that you are heir to all the good in the universe.

Take time to feel the love, the glory, the abundance, the beauty, the presence that is within you. You could possess all the things around you that you think you need and still be very unhappy, very lonely, very miserable and very much in want. The reason is that *things* do not make us happy.

Things give us temporary relief. Things distract our attention for a time, but if our real needs are not fulfilled, they will come back and gnaw at us like a deep unsatisfied hunger. We find that what we need is a consciousness which brings us into the fullness of truth—the truth of our divine inheritance and the abundance which is always ours. The first step is the step in consciousness, the developing awareness of our oneness with Originating Good.

Jesus said, "I am the way, the truth, and the life." You are the way, the truth and the life unto your own happiness, your own abundance. That which is yours by divine right must come to you by way of your own consciousness. It is already within you awaiting your recognition.

How do you recognize this? How do you bring it into your experience? By looking to your thoughts and your feelings. You cannot demonstrate the opposite of what you think and feel. If you feel you are a pauper, you will not draw abundance to you. Life will respond in like manner to your thoughts and feelings.

If, on the other hand, you begin to feel that you are rich in ideas, rich in love, rich in creativity, rich in expression, beautiful good will begin to manifest in your life.

Say to yourself:

My cup of riches runneth over. I feel the flow of my good through me. I feel rich in all that I experience. I have a wonderful feeling about life and the abundance which is mine. I am rich in consciousness.

Do not think that ten years from now your good will manifest. Think in terms of now. The moment you put a magnet in proximity to that which is like unto itself, it begins to attract.

There is no time-lapse. The moment you attain a rich conscious-ness, your good is attracted to you. Your life is enriched.

Think to yourself, "My good is here right now. Every possible answer exists in the nowness. Every possible demon-stration is here in the nowness. Every need is met in the nowness."

You see, life belongs to the one who recognizes that he or she is life. Life belongs to you. You were not created to suffer. I cannot believe that anyone or anything in the vastness of the universe was created to suffer. The Infinite does not suffer and we are one with the Infinite. I see the universe as a grand idea which is constantly expanding and we are expanding with it.

If we suffer or if we are impoverished, that experience comes from the way we use our minds. It comes from our own thinking. We are as rich as we feel. It is our thinking and our attitude that make us rich or poor. It is our feeling of lack or our feeling of abundance.

Know today that everything you need already exists right now in consciousness. Your good is right here, all around you and within you. Accept in consciousness that which is yours by divine right.

The gift has been made. Before you call, you are answered. That is, the answer already awaits you. When you make a demand upon life in the right consciousness, then you receive. I firmly believe that all is in mind. That is why I can definitely say that your good is already in mind. Your health already exists. Your need is already fulfilled, but for you to receive, you must come into rapport with that which is yours.

Say to yourself right now:

I know that my good is already at hand. To receive my good, I think as Mind thinks. I know as Universal Intelligence knows. I act as the unlimited Power acts. I

94

move into the consciousness of at-one-ment and everything falls into place.

You must enlarge your consciousness. You must get the feeling David expressed in the Twenty-third Psalm when he said, "The Lord is my shepherd. I shall not want...."

When you know that Infinite Intelligence is always your provider, you will know you cannot want. You cannot lack. If, however, you condemn what you have, if you see only limitation, and if you do nothing but criticize, your good will diminish rather than increase. Condemnation restricts. Praise and blessings increase.

If you are not demonstrating your good, you are out of step with life. Listen to what life is trying to tell you. Know that the Power is within you. Stop looking at the lack. Stop blaming and start praising.

Do not try to change your life by changing effects. Do not try to change things, people, circumstances, or your bank account. Concentrate on consciousness first and when you have a rich consciousness, your outer world will begin to reflect this consciousness. You will begin to demonstrate your good.

Say:

All good is mine today and every day. I accept my good by divine right of consciousness. In this conscious oneness with the Infinite, I know that I can never want for any good thing.

A New You

Don't let your assets remain locked within you. Be fired with the recognition that the potential to be and the potential to do are right within you, and that life is what you make it. Anytime you align yourself with the Infinite, new avenues of expression and creativity open for you.

Any day you can close the past behind you and begin a fresh experience. How do you do begin anew? You do not do it by recounting all of your sorrows. You do not do it by recounting all your losses. You do it by letting go of the past. You let go of the past completely and look to the unblemished present as if it were a beautiful, blank page upon which you can write anything you choose.

You do it by realizing that there is nothing in your future which is against you. The way is an open road which you can travel with great joy. It is filled with many opportunities, and many marvelous experiences await you.

All people, whether they be writers, artists, business people, or homemakers, are sometimes faced with feelings of helplessness. That usually means that they are letting former disappointments and negative events influence them. They—and all of us—need to realize that this is not yesterday. It is today, fresh and new and ready to be lived in the now.

If this is a fresh day and you are fresh in it, it is not too late. It is not too late to be successful. It is not too late to be happy. It is not too late to clean the slate and write a new story. "But," you cry out, "I am broken in heart and in spirit." You may have a heartache. You may hurt, but you are never broken in spirit, for Spirit can never be broken. It can appear broken, but it is only covered over by our hurt and negativity.

Know today that life itself knows no sorrow. Life is progressive. It will not be imprisoned in the past. It is offering you change at all times. Wherever you are and wherever your loved ones are, change is taking place all the time. Sometimes the changes are not necessarily what we want, but when we view them from a large enough perspective, we can see that they are for the better.

Get the marvelous feeling of newness, of starting all over again. You can dig in and do what you have always wanted to do, as long as you know that the Spirit which is within you is the divine Spirit and it cannot be broken and it cannot be hurt. Determine to let this Spirit come forth with great joy.

Life cannot be cramped. We may cramp our style of living, but life itself cannot be cramped. Life is free-flowing creativity. Often we try to force it into molds that restrict its flow and when we do this, we have trouble. We cannot mold life into that which is against its nature.

Claim your good. Claim that which is yours by divine right. Claim your happiness. Claim your health. Claim your success. When you claim what is yours by divine right, you are not claiming that which belongs to another. Nor are you holding onto the idea of the money you lost last year or the investment which did not pay off.

When you claim your good, you forget your mistakes. When you claim your good, you forget the injuries and hurts you have received. You forget the disappointments you have experienced. Why? Because you cannot really claim your good in this new day and at the same time be overwhelmed with memories of the past. You can't look in two different directions at the same time. You carry over into this new day only those things that are going to be an asset to you in this new beginning.

Realize right now that whatever troubles you have experienced, whatever difficulties you have gone through, can be chalked up to experience and education. You can learn from them but do not hold onto them. Like Jacob, who wrestled all night with the angel and would not let go until the angel blessed him, you can hold onto your hurts, disappointments, heartaches and problems long enough to let them educate you. You can say, "What is there in this experience that I can learn? What can it teach me? How can I profit from it?" Then you must let these experiences go.

If you chalk them up to education, they can benefit you. You can say, "I have learned what I do not want to do. I have learned what I do not want to experience again. I have learned what I do not want to see repeated. I am through with it. I let it go."

Enter into a new state of consciousness by knowing that past negative experiences do not determine your future. You are going into a new area of livingness. It is not too late. You are not too old. Life within you has no age and it flows forward in waves of creativity and growth at all times. Get in step with it today. Feel the limitless power within you.

Yes, today can be the beginning of a new year, a new life and a new you. Your foot is on the threshold of a new life the moment you decide it shall be so.

Say:

My mind is flaming with creativity. My heart is warm with love. I let this be the first day of a new year in my life. I see it as a fresh, white page upon which I choose what shall be written.

Chapter Six

~~~

A Bright
New Beginning

The caterpillar does all the work and the butterfly gets all the publicity.

—George Carlin

～～～

The future is purchased by the present.

—Samuel Johnson

Subconsciously we set our own terms with life. We make an unwritten contract with it. We set our own limits and we restrict our own possibilities. In this contract the so-called "fine print" is sometimes so fine that we cannot read it, but it makes an impact on our lives just the same.

Let us be aware of this impact today and come into a new beginning. Let us begin to think in new terms, feel in a new way, take on new attitudes, and view life in entirely new and different terms. Let us make a new contract with life and cancel the old one, making sure that the fine print does not unconsciously influence us in negative and limiting ways.

Begin to think in terms of newness when it comes to health, prosperity, relationships, and business. Instead of looking at life and feeling that it has bound you in a limiting contract, realize that in your subconscious mind, you agreed to the terms of the contract with which you are complying.

Both the conscious and subconscious sides of your mind are reflected in your daily living. Your five senses report to you the state of affairs on the surface; they are like weather vanes that indicate the way things are going. What the five senses communicate has first been screened through the subconsious and conscious mind. This screening is such an insidious process that we may find ourselves experiencing certain conditions without knowing what caused them—which is a powerful reason to draw up a new contract in consciousness, to always be looking for and thinking of expansion and newness in every phase of our living and not become set in old patterns.

Even if you move to a new town or take a new position, you will find that no real change takes place until you change in consciousness. You must uplift your thinking. You can do this right now—today. You can tear up the old contract.

Your contract with life can be as great as you can imagine it to be. According to the condition of your consciousness, life gives to you. You are never outside the operation of your good, but like the employee who toils away at a mediocre job year after year when there are many possibilities for advancement, we are sometimes too embroiled in sameness to see new possibilities.

Remember that no change should be permanent. Any newness will become old if you are not constantly desirous of improvement. When you cease to look for the new, crystallization sets in and you become brittle; you may then break under the little strains and minor stresses which should only challenge you—if you are flexible and ready for the next step forward.

Remember that last year or several years ago, perhaps, you made a new contract with life. Everything was to be different, and it was—for a while—but you kept renewing the same contract until it became dated and outworn. It no longer fit the needs of today's living. It isn't that you made a wrong or detrimental contract with life but that you have outgrown the conditions of that contract.

Each January we celebrate the New Year. What a wonderful event! It brings to our mind the fact that we can always begin anew. We can always make new decisions about our living. Annually, if only briefly, we review our old contract and make new resolutions. We may not keep every one of them, but at least we have been somewhat stirred to newness. New beginnings, new possibilities lure us.

It is significant that in our culture New Year's Day comes in the depth of winter, before the signatures of spring are evident. So, in the depth of winter in consciousness, if you feel the need for change, know that as winter comes, spring cannot be far behind. Just as spring changes the landscape of winter to greenness and flowers, so will your decisions to change move you out of mental dormancy into the regeneration of life.

Remember that the seasons roll around, and the newness of spring becomes the fullness of summer and the fullness of summer becomes the harvest of autumn and then goes into a wintering phase. When this happens in your life, you have made the circuit.

Now is the time to make a new contract with life. It is time to plant anew. You must take the best seeds of your harvest and plant them in new and enriched mental soil so your next crop will be an abundant one. Your life must not be impoverished through planting in the same old worn-out soil of consciousness.

Say to yourself:

I make a new contract with life today–completely new. I delete the insidious fine print that was subconsciously causing me trouble and draw up a new contract, acceptable to the spirit. I do not depend upon agreements I made with life ten years ago, or even a year ago. Today's living demands new terms, new conditions, and greater dividends. I update my contract with life to meet the challenges of today in effective and enriching ways.

103

Feasting and Fasting

If this is to be a new beginning, there must be a termination of the old. We cannot enter into newness as long as we insist on carrying with us thoughts, feelings, and images that are not productive of our highest good. If we want to advance physically, mentally and spiritually, we must let go of everything that may be holding us back.

As long as we dwell in the darkness of the past, we cannot see the light that illumines our present—light which represents truth, love, understanding and new life.

We must come into a clear consciousness of the light and do as St. Paul did. He said, "Forgetting those things which are behind, I press on to the mark of my high calling." What do you want to cross out of your life and what do you want to add to your life today? Whatever it is, you must arrive at the point of forgetting those things that are behind and press forward into newness.

Say to yourself right now:
I want to experience greater health in my life. I want to experience a feeling of inner tranquility. I want to experience fulfillment. I am willing to forget the past and press forward into this new consciousness of life.

When the quickening of Spirit occurs in your consciousness, life will take on a deeper dimension. But the capacity to forgive and forget must be exercised in order for this deepening to happen. Work with the idea of light, and the cleansing process will take place within you.

Once you cleanse your mind and your heart of that which you no longer want in your new life, you must exercise discipline. Every time the old wants intrude again, you must evict it and focus your mind on the new, bringing it back again and again to the goals you have set for yourself.

As you go through the process of cleansing and disciplining, do not worry or be concerned about what others think. The important thing is that you are noticing the changes which are taking place in your consciousness.

There is a mighty Power within you. There is an unchangeable Truth within you. There is that Spirit of life, light and love within you, and the more you feast on these ideas and fast from old, corrosive ones, the closer you will come to experiencing the life you desire.

Say to yourself right now, "Everything that I do, I do with the realization that I work with Infinite Mind. I work with the Truth." Feel that you are the light and are walking in the light. Acknowledge that within you is a living temple which is the holy of holies. In this holy of holies dwells a beautiful Presence. This Presence is your life, your intelligence, and your gateway to something new and different each day of your life.

In this consciousness, you know that underneath you are the "everlasting arms." You know you are being cared for and carried forward, as long as you "let go," as long as you know that all things are possible through perseverance and adherence to divine principle and that you do not have to continue to walk in darkness.

How good your life can be if you will fast from the darkness of the past and feast on the Presence within you. The light will shine all about you, and your way will be made clear and straight.

Say:

*I separate the darkness from the light in my life and walk
in the light.*

The Power Is Here

Let's begin today with a new certainty, a new confidence. From time to time we redecorate our homes, buy a later model car, and change our style of dress. Just as important is our need to acquire new ideas about ourselves. If our thinking is outmoded, we must bring it up to date, not hesitating to eliminate old ways of thinking from our consciousness. Let's permit ourselves to expand into a new awareness and a new experience of life.

It takes strength to change our lives. It takes courage to break with the old and instigate something new, but if we will turn quietly within and trust the strength that is within us, it will support us.

Wishing will not get you where you want to go. Stop wishing and declare the word of Truth. Stop hoping and declare! If you want a new beginning, speak your word for a new beginning. If you want peace, speak your word of peace. If you want freedom, speak your word for freedom. Speak, declare, decree what you want to experience in your life and then rest quietly in confidence, knowing that it will manifest. Let words of truth ever widen your greater expression of life.

I cannot say often enough that nothing is too good to be true. We so easily accept the negative side of things and think the good is not always for us. Why not for us? Whom else could it be for? Accept the idea of good in your life. Accept the idea of your life-expression becoming better and better all the time, instead of diminishing.

The Infinite has already given everything that can be given. When we pray, we should remember this. We should know that we are not praying for a deity to do something, for others to move into action. We pray to align ourselves with the divine right action which is taking place at all times. We pray to bring ourselves into a state of quietness, confidence and strength. We pray to come to the point of acceptance.

You do not have to wait for the power to move in. The power is within you right now. You are already using it. Your prayers do not generate power; they only put you in a position of realizing that it is already here, already working.

Suppose a physicist had to wait for energy to move in. The physicist knows that energy *is*. In the same way truth is, love is, and life is. Just as the room you are in is filled with air, so are you filled with all of the life, love and power there is.

Life is activity. The invisible Reality is creativity in action at all times. Do not wait for Spirit to move in; move out into expression. Realize that Divine Mind has manifested already, and the next step is yours. Life cannot be analyzed by the human mind. It is of the Spirit and it must be experienced, not figured out. Life is what you are. It is the breath of Spirit being made manifest through you. If you could but realize this, what a multitude of cares and worries you would drop by the wayside!

There are no barriers between you and the infinite Life Force, between you and whatever healing you need.

If your world looks like a mess to you, look to your erroneous thoughts. Know you have perpetuated something in ignorance that can be corrected and cleared up by a new insight, a new learning, a new realization. Begin to put your mental house in order.

Your good exists now. It is within reach of you now. A wholesome, robust life is yours now. The well of your good can never run dry.

Each day you should work from the unlimited nature of your being. Say to yourself right now:

I work in the consciousness of truth and I work with love.
I am unlimited in my spiritual nature. My mind is

unlimited. The life within me is unlimited. My creativity is
unlimited. My ideas are unlimited. The beauty around me
and within me is unlimited. I am unlimited in every respect.

Do not feel that you are going to have to use a lot of will power to change your life. What you do need to use is "willingness" power. Can you look at fear today and completely loose it and let it go? Out of fear and ignorance all the other negatives breed. Let go of your fears, your hurts, your distrust of life and heal your thoughts of lack, separation, and inharmony by knowing that infinite Power is already within you, acting for you and simply awaiting your acceptance of it.

Michaelangelo, when he sculpted a beautiful piece of statuary, took the marble and chipped away what he did not want. He brought forth that which he saw as beautiful in the marble. You can eliminate from your life that which you do not want and bring forth the beautiful Presence which is within you.

What are you waiting for? Get into the nowness. Get that now feeling. Know that this is the time of your transformation. Every day can bring you closer to the Presence within you. Every day can reveal more of your good to you.

The next time you feel confused or angry, remember, "In quietness and confidence is my strength." Stand in the midst of the turmoil or pain and decree the Truth. You may not be able to do this one hundred percent the first time, but practice the Presence and it will become real to you. A house is built brick by brick. A life is built thought by thought. You can build a stately mansion or a poor hovel. It all depends upon your consciousness and your acceptance of the power within you.

Say:

I speak my word for a new beginning of my life. All of life
and its fullest potentials are within me at this moment. I
realize this and let them come forth into expression.

108

Release the Past

You are a creative expression of an infinite Intelligence. You may not be fully aware of your talents or the depth of your creativity, but the fact remains that you are a creative individual.

Your mind is creative. It is filled with ideas. It is an individualization of the same Mind that created the whole universe, that brought everything into being and sustains and maintains everything. The Divine Mind is infinite and no matter how much it fans out, it never depletes itself. Since you are an offspring of this Mind, the qualities of the Infinite must be within you.

Your unfoldment of consciousness cannot come from somebody else any more than the unfoldment of a rose can be forced. The rose must unfold itself, petal by petal. A geranium cannot take pity on a rose and say, "The thing is stuck. I had better help it out." The rose must unfold itself. No matter how much the geranium might want to help the rose, the rose must reveal its own individuality.

You, at whatever stage of growth you are, must unfold your own individuality. You must recognize, "I am creative. I am using this wonderful, infinite Mind. I am one with this infinite Power. I must unfold the ideas within myself. I must unfold the beauty of my true nature. I must unfold love and I am the only one who can do these things for myself."

When you are ready for your unfoldment, it will come. When you are ready to release your old way of living for a better way, that, too, will come about. When you are ready to cease being an angry individual, a petty individual, a hurt individual, you will begin to unfold your true nature.

Feel yourself as a living branch on the tree of life. The life in this tree is your life. The nourishment in this tree is your

109

nourishment. The creativity in this tree is your creativity. You are a part of life, just as the branch is a part of the tree. Know that you have the potential to unfold in many beautiful ways. Consciously work on unfolding the creativity within you.

Decide that every day you will expose yourself to something new. Do not hesitate to try something that you have not done before. Do not judge yourself by what you were last year. Today is the time in which you are living and experiencing. If you drag the past along, you will go at life halfheartedly. Go at it full blast. When you are half-hearted, you must admit that you are only half-alive. Come into the fullness of life now.

In the springtime the ground is prepared for new plantings. Everything is cleared away that might hinder the growth of the new plants. In releasing, you do the same thing in your life. If you want to plant something new, you must prepare the soil of mind. You must make room for the newness. If someone gave you a beautiful new plant from a nursery, you would not jam it in a pot with several other plants. You would give it a pot of its own. You would give it growing room. The same is true if you get a new idea about yourself. You must make room in your consciousness for that idea and then you must implant it there so it can grow.

Life should be an exciting, exhilarating experience, not something that is lukewarm and halfhearted. We should be functioning on all cylinders, not just one or two. If you live life fully, you will have your ups and downs. So what! You are living. You are in command of your life. You are experiencing. You are undertaking something new all the time.

Isn't it a marvelous feeling to know that you are not cut off from your good but that you are centered in life, that you swim in your good, and that the only reason you do not experience the creativity within you is that you do not recognize it is there? You can awake. You can begin to unfold the infinite creativity within you.

As you do so, you will begin to choose the thoughts you think with more care, for they are your first step toward unfoldment. You are the thinker in your world. No one can think for you. What you think is what you will get. So choose wisely. Feel yourself as a pipeline through which all the life force, the creativity, the fresh, vital ideas flow. Let your excitement about life stir up the gifts and talents within you.

If there is something in your life that is holding you back and making you unhappy, you do not have to tolerate it. You do not have to remain where you are in consciousness. There is always something you can do about it. Why sentence yourself to halfhearted living when all of life is knocking on your door?

Say:

I release from my consciousness those thoughts, feelings, and attitudes which have been holding me back. I stir up the gift of new life within me.

Clearing the Consciousness

Jesus taught that we should not put our hand to the plow and look back. What did he mean by that? What is a plow for? It is for breaking up the old, hard ground and preparing it for renewal. If we are trying to plow ahead of us and are looking back over our shoulder, what kind of furrow will we plow?

When you are ready to break up the crystallized ideas in your mind and prepare your consciousness for newness, do not look back. Look ahead. Jesus said we cannot expand while looking back and holding on to the old at the same time. We must let go of that which is behind us. We are here to grow and to move ahead.

Ask yourself today, "Am I ready to take the plow in hand

111

and break up my old thinking, my old habit patterns, and all of the old feelings I have? Am I ready to release the old image of myself and see myself in a new light? If I am ready to do this, what am I going to plant after I have done the plowing?" You must be ready to plant new ideas, new thoughts and new feelings, and not look back to what has been. Let go of old habit patterns of thoughts and feelings. The kingdom of heaven is within you and this is where you expand. Neither Moses nor Jesus would ever have accomplished anything in their lives if they had looked only at appearances.

Both of these dynamic wayshowers knew that right where they were, Omniscient Spirit always was. They knew that the Universal Presence was the source of their power and strength, and that Mind was their intelligence. When we begin to incorporate love, faith and strength into our lives, our experiences will change.

Isn't it interesting that it only takes one rotten apple to spoil the whole lot? It only takes one thought to spoil our day and put us down in the dumps or to lift us up. All of us make great strides when we are willing to take the responsibility for our own consciousness.

Often we want our freedom, but we cannot be free from a problem or a situation until we are free within ourselves. One of the greatest gifts we can give ourselves is to set ourselves free in consciousness. We need to set anyone free who has offended us or turned against us or disappointed us. We need to set anyone free who has ill-treated us and let them go. There is no greater reward than the one we will experience in consciousness.

Begin to eliminate from your awareness any blocks which might be holding you back. Be bold enough to claim your good. Be conscious enough of your true selfhood to feel deserving of the best. Get out of the unhappiness trap. Sometimes the only way you can accomplish this is to take an inventory of your complaints and find out what areas in your thinking might be giving you trouble.

We must stop the habit of complaining and begin to seek out things to praise. We complain about many things: our job, the housework, the children, the way the car runs. Perhaps the dog doesn't react the way we think he should. If we checked our thoughts and feelings for only one day, we would be surprised at the nagging, complaining thoughts that we generate.

You do not know what the remainder of this day holds for you, nor do I. It can hold more of the same or it can be new and different. It can be an adventure or an endurance contest. It can be full of grievances or full of joy. We do not have to know the details, but we do know the trend our lives are taking. If we insist on looking down and not up, that is the trend our lives will take.

Today, look at life unafraid. There is no situation you cannot overcome. Claim your identity with Spirit. Claim your unity with Life. Be spiritually alive and there is no situation you cannot overcome in a most beautiful way.

Say:

Today I find new ways of doing things, new ways of exploring the creativity within me. I am open to the spiritual aliveness within myself and become an open channel through which the life of the Infinite works.

The Constancy of Inconstancy

We are always seeking a balance, and yet, when this balance is reached, it is only the springboard which propels us into a new imbalance and the cycle repeats itself all over again. In other words, none of us remains constant. If we did we would stagnate. We would not grow.

Never feel that you must remain fixed and constant, or that you have to be tomorrow what you are today. Some people never want a marriage to change or a loved one to change, yet without change there can be no growth. Without growth the most beautiful of marriages will die. Without unfoldment, love will wither and cease to bloom.

You could not remain constant even if you tried. The kind of constancy I am referring to is remaining with the status quo. I am not saying we should be untrue to those we love but that in this life there should be growth.

If we are set in our ways, our thinking, and our attitudes, we become brittle and we break here and there. We break in our health. We break in our happiness. We break in our relationships. We break where our abundance is concerned. If we break, the process of growth ceases.

The only person you can ever change is you and the only growing you can do is for yourself. Know, today, that the root of all reality is within you and that no matter how entrenched in difficulty and confusion you are, no matter how deeply disturbed you are, no matter how you are churning inwardly, you can begin anew. You can build on the reality within you. You can think creatively. You can grow.

If we are in trouble, we have set a trap and caught ourselves in it. It seems ridiculous that we would do this, but we do. Ask yourself today how many traps you have let yourself get caught in. Anger? Resentment? Hopelessness? Belittlement? There are scores of them and we trick ourselves into forgetting that we are constantly baiting our own traps with erroneous beliefs that bring us disappointment.

There is nothing more beautiful for you to know than that

you are a part of a cosmic energy. The whole universe is part of this energy and it runs and functions in absolute harmony. Know today that if you feel outside of the circle of good, it is only because you have lost sight of your unity with all things. You have let yourself get caught up in separation.

Today, grab hold of life. Look at the whole picture on a wide screen of livingness. See this cosmic energy and power as your own. Know that it is centered in you and that it is centered in every individual in the universe. Since it is a harmonizing power, it can bring harmony into your experience. It can enable you to think at a new level, feel at a new level, and live at a new level.

Take a moment right now to get close to that center. Feel the invisible Presence within you. Feel the cosmic energy filling you. Feel infinite love flowing through you. Feel the power that is within you, filling every pore of your being. As it moves, know that it is flushing out every bit of ugliness and negativity in your life. It is removing every feeling of upsetness. It is dissolving the fatigue. It is moving out the feeling that others have let you down. It is moving out every hurt. It is moving out everything that is not productive of your good.

Continue to feel this Presence and Power pour through you. Feel it as streamers of light. Feel the intelligence pouring in. Feel this power bringing with it everything you need, flushing out that which you do not need. You are not wrestling with anything outside of you. You are developing the consciousness that there is something in you right now—something shining, something cleansing—that is changing your life for the better.

Say to yourself:

In Spirit I live and move and have my being. Wherever I am, it is. Whatever it is, I am. Whenever I call upon it, it responds. I have but to align my consciousness to its infinite flow.

Today is the day for you to claim your good. Today is the day for you to throw the traps away. Today is the day for you to recognize the reality within you. Today is the day for you to let go of all that does not matter and let yourself grow.

Say to yourself right now:

Today, I claim the consciousness that is mine. Today, I claim the joy that is mine. Today, I claim the peace that is mine. Today, I claim the harmony that is mine.

Claim these things. They are here for you. When you accept them, you are not taking from another. You are not diminishing the supply.

So many times we view ourselves as insignificant. We see ourselves as small and powerless. We see ourselves as being separate and alone. Begin to realize today that the whole universe is centered within you and the power that is universal is yours also. This is why love is so important. It bears this creative energy within it. It is a creative energy of itself. I believe it is so creative that it can change us mentally, emotionally, and physically. It can energize and heal whatever needs energy and healing in our lives. It can literally transform us.

Say:

I let the energy of life pour through me with all its purity and invigorating power. I let love sweep away all that is unlike itself in my life today.

Chapter Seven

~~~

You Are Free to Choose

The world is before you and you need not take it or leave it as it was when you came in.

–James Baldwin

~~~

May I ask you a highly personal question? It's what life does all the time.

–Kurt Vonnegut

*N*o matter how many times we declare that we are free externally, until we truly believe it internally we are constantly placing ourselves in bondage. The attainment of inner freedom comes first.

Often we think that someone is interfering with our freedom. We feel hampered and hemmed in. We feel pushed into a corner. But no one has the power to do that to us. No one can make us a prisoner, if we realize that we are endowed with absolute freedom.

Even if we are behind prison bars, we do not have to be prisoners in our consciousness. As the poet said, "Stone walls do not a prison make nor iron bars a cage." Why? Because we can be free in spirit, free in mind.

Infinite Mind is within us and it is serene at all times. It is never disturbed. It is never hampered. It is never imprisoned. If we feel imprisoned, we are hampering the expression of our freedom with our own thoughts.

Do not mistake serenity for passivity. You can be serene

and at the same time very active. There is nothing passive about life. It is electrically alive. Life sings and dances; it bounces, it surges, it tingles, and it grows. Even in its quietness and apparent stillness, it is vibrantly alive. If life is alive in this way, so are you, for you are a part of its aliveness.

Today, with every breath you breathe, know that you are radiantly, vibrantly alive. See and feel yourself as one with the goodness of life. Unify with it in consciousness as you are already unified with it in truth.

You have never been separate from the whole. The more you are able to relate to the whole, the more complete your life will be. You will see that you are unrestricted and endowed with the freedom of Spirit and that spiritual law then gives you more freedom, not less.

Tension (and is tension not a restraint in its own way, a holding back?) has to stem from something. Naturally, it cannot stem from First Cause because that is absolute peace, love, harmony and flow. Therefore, tension must be an indication of mental and emotional separation. It must be mental confusion and a fear of loss.

Such uptightness causes us to feel physical discomfort. We attribute this to our physical nerves, but it is not our nerves that bother us. We are bothering our nerves! There is nothing wrong with the nervous system. It is one of the finest, most sensitive systems within the human body. It is a system of intelligence. It operates harmoniously and interrelates with the other body systems.

It is we who, in our fear and anticipation of loss and separation, interfere with the perfect working of this system. When our nerves are on edge, we should explore what thoughts or feelings are troubling us.

Beyond those thoughts and feelings, deep within us, is

absolute peace. This area is within every individual. It is within you. It is not something you create. It is something you always have available to you, no matter how much turmoil there is on the surface. Jesus said, "Peace I leave with you, my peace I give unto you." He was speaking of the Christ Consciousness within you, which is always at peace.

Now you might say, "This is fine when I am at home, but when I leave my home, there is anything but peace where I go." If you go about your daily living with a beautiful consciousness of peace you will carry peace with you. If, on the other hand, you carry hostility with you, that is what you will attract wherever you go. We create our hostilities, but we do not create peace—we recognize it. Suppose, for instance, you meet someone who is just itching for a good argument. If your mind is in perfect peace, this person cannot get a ripple of an argument out of you.

There is one infinite Intelligence, there is one infinite Spirit, and there is one infinite Life. If Divine Mind is all in all, then we must be in its love and peace, and we must be in its truth and light. Invisible and intangible as they are to the outer senses, they are here and we must reach within ourselves and bring them to the surface. We must blend the expression of love and peace into our outer expression of life.

We do not need to create spiritual assets; we only have to reach into consciousness and find them. When turmoil rages on the surface, it might help to remember that on the ocean when the waves roll high in every direction and the whitecaps are frothing, underneath the water is calm. The storm can only ruffle the surface. It cannot disturb the inner depths of the ocean.

The same is true of your life. No matter how chaotic the storm or upheaval appears, you can move through any and all conditions with serenity because peace abides in the center of your being. Whether you experience freedom or bondage depends on how you approach life.

Say to yourself today:

I am free with the freedom of Spirit. Nothing can bind me in consciousness. I am at peace within and nothing can disturb this deep peace within me. I know that beneath every storm is the deep calm of harmonious life. I know that whatever seems to hamper me or hem me in is an illusion of the senses or of my human mind. Because I am free within, I am, indeed, free in all areas. I reach in and touch this level of consciousness within me today and I experience perfect peace and freedom.

No Evil

There is no power except Divine Power, and the Divine which is Infinite Love cannot be the author of evil. If we deal with Reality, there is no evil. This idea is difficult to accept at times, because people, with their dual thinking, have produced many effects that we call evil, and we see them expressed abundantly in the world around us.

As long as we give power to anything except infinite First Cause, we are not centered in divine awareness. We have not realized what Reality truly is. To say that Infinite Love is all and then live in fear of evil is a contradiction. To say that there is only one power and that is Divine Power and then to speak of the devil or some other force having control over us is giving power to that which has no power.

Sometimes when we are in very difficult situations, it is not easy to believe that there is no evil. The testimony seems to be all about us and appears to be affecting our lives in many ways.

This is because we are seeing double. We are not dealing with Truth.

In reality there is no evil, but in the man-made world it looms huge, like a many-headed Hydra. If we try to get rid of it by fighting it, two new heads grow where the old head was cut off, and we are worse off than we were before.

Many things need changing in the world of appearances, but attacking them directly will get us nowhere. When we do so, we are giving them power. We are saying, "Here is something evil, something wrong. I must fight it. I must eliminate it." So we fight it. Maybe the problem goes underground, but it will pop up somewhere else. It is not really eliminated at all. As long as the attention is on the problem, it will remain.

Only when you turn your attention from the problem, knowing there is only one Power, do things begin to change for the better. You will experience evil to the degree that you lose sight of reality. If you put air in a balloon, it gets bigger and bigger, but if you let the air out, it becomes smaller and smaller. If you put attention on a problem, the same thing happens.

The eyes cannot see evil, the ears cannot hear evil, and the lips cannot speak evil, unless you give power to evil in your consciousness. It all stems from consciousness. Now, I am not denying that the appearance of what we call evil exists in the world about us. It does, but it is humanly made and humans give it power through the attention they invest in it.

Infinite Intelligence is not the author of evil and no one and no thing can work against you if you accept fully and completely that there is only one Power. What permits adverse conditions to thrive in your life is your giving power to something other than the One Power.

As long as you recognize that no person, no group and no thing can work against you, you are anchored in the Infinite

Power and are not giving authority to anything else. As long, however, as you believe evil to be a thing of itself, then it remains real to you.

All the evil which exists is the evil of humankind, not evil of a divine origin. All of the suffering which exists is the suffering of humankind, not the suffering of divine Love. What must we do then? We must move into the consciousness of Reality. We must turn away from the duality of believing in two powers and anchor to the one unifying Power.

Today, if you are suffering from any form of evil, begin to dissipate it with the thought, "There is no ultimate reality to this. Good is the only reality." This is taking quite a leap, because the world speaks otherwise and even your own senses suggest that evil is real. This step is easier if you realize that a negative experience is something that is happening only as an experience, but it is not ultimate reality.

Each of us, in our own way, opens the door through which evil, of our own creation, comes into our life. Every time we become fearful, we are believing in duality. Every fear has its basis in dual thinking. Every experience contrary to our good has its basis in duality.

Say to yourself at such a time:
I will get back in principle. I know there is only one power.
There is only oneness. I refuse to see duality.

Every fear we experience is a move from unity to duality. When we are filled with fear and the world is crumbling about us, at that moment we have to say, "There must be a basis for this fear and that basis must be that I am off-center. I am recognizing good and bad, when in reality there is only the Good. I will get back into the consciousness of oneness."

We protest that we believe in only one Power and then we see health and sickness, abundance and want, good and evil, happiness and unhappiness, light and darkness. As long as we are seeing double, then we will experience double in our lives. As long as we are seeing the pairs of opposites, we are not truly anchored in unity and oneness.

If, in consciousness, we could rise above both good and evil, it might be easier to understand the unity of all life. Life is. Mind is. Divine Mind is not good or bad. Infinite Intelligence is perfect and exists in this perfection.

Say to yourself:

I let my consciousness be lifted above duality. I let myself see the wholeness, the completeness, the unity of all life, and choose to abide in this oneness. No matter what I experience in the world of apparent facts, I know that in reality there is only one Power, one Life, one supreme Intelligence. I center in this oneness.

Changing the Subconscious Mind

If you are programmed for trouble, that is what you will get. If you are on the alert for trouble, trouble will find you. If you go to work tomorrow morning and feel that you are working with a bunch of troublemakers, what will you meet? A bunch of troublemakers. Or if you go to school and feel that your teacher likes the whole class but is out to get you, then the teacher will be out to get you.

Life can only react to us as we feel and believe.

We can never change others. We can only change our very own point of view. It is remarkable, but when we change our point of view, life moves with us in that new direction.

What we experience depends on us—not on what others are doing to us, but on what we are doing to ourselves.

Get into your consciousness today that Infinite Intelligence created you in its image and likeness and that you are loved. Love yourself. Feel adequate in every situation. Feel unified with the whole. Never feel that you are on the outside of the world looking in.

Ask yourself today: "How am I programmed? How am I programmed subconsciously? Am I programmed to experience problems, tensions, pressures, and worries?" If so, it will do no good to try to run away from them. Believe me, you will find pressures and tensions and worry wherever you go. If you are experiencing them where you are, you will take them with you.

Someone else says, "If I could only find an island and just get lost!" Is that living? No. I believe we can be at the very hub of activity and yet know the presence of peace. We grow in the midst of challenges. What do we need to do, then, to experience peace? We need to reprogram our subconscious mind.

Many of us have invisible crutches and they are much more pernicious than the kinds of crutches we can see. For example, many of us lean on other people. But this need not be, for within each of us is an omnipresent Power. When we realize that, we come into a new birth of freedom and learn to rely only upon our spiritual self.

You do not have to be a sponge and absorb all the negativity around you. You can reflect the supremacy of your inner spirit. If you feel inadequate, you have built up your inadequacies. When you are uptight, you are the one who has let the pressures build up within you. If you go deep enough into your beingness, you will find a place of peace.

You are here to become a spiritual giant. You can draw from an infinite source as much good as you can encompass in your consciousness. You do not need to run from life or to hide from it. You can stand steadfast in the realization that within you are peace, dignity, poise, serenity and love.

Program yourself for health. Program yourself for love. Establish firmly in your subconscious mind that whenever you think of your body you think of it in terms of health. Program yourself for opportunity so whenever you consider your future all you can see are great possibilities. Program yourself for a marvelous consciousness of abundance so you are not caught up in lack and limitation. Develop the feeling that every time you spend money you are spending it from unlimited abundance. Whenever you think of money, think of it as continuous abundance and you will cancel out lack. Use the ideas in this book to program yourself spiritually to experience the sufficiency in you, to experience the best in you.

Program yourself particularly to overcome a feeling that you are isolated and separated. Feel that you are one with Universal Intelligence, one with an infinite Source, and you will advance in life. We become conditioned to negativity and fear, but let's come into a new awareness of ourselves today. Let us recondition ourselves and really know the truth of our being instead of plunging into life with our inner eyes closed. Let us become aware of divine Power within us, of divine Love, of Truth. Let us know that negatively conditioned thinking is now being wiped out completely and we are coming into a new consciousness, a new beingness.

Condition your subconscious mind right now to focus on possibility. Image only love, and don't get caught in the past. Release the past and let it go. Many of us have invisible crutches and we lean on these invisible crutches, when we need to lean on the Truth. Depend solely on Truth and know that underneath you is your ever-present support. This is the only way to arrive at a new birth of freedom. When we lean on the spirituality of our being we lean on the wonderful truth that divine perfection in us, as us, expresses itself through us. The next time you get caught in something which appears to be absolutely terrible, when confusion is all around you, become very quiet and declare that peace permeates the situation. You have the power within you to bring forth a new experience as you declare peace in the midst of chaos.

You do not have to absorb all the negativity around you. Reflect the supremacy of your inner spirit. Build up a feeling of infinite love. Whenever you are tense, let go of the pressure and find the peace that is within you. Feel that you are a spiritual giant drawing directly from the omnipotent Source. Don't run from life; don't hide. Stand steadfast in a realization of the Presence. Get into that beautiful consciousness today. Let your light shine in the world and live your life in power, in strength, in courage, and with conviction. Live it knowing that Infinite Intelligence is the source of your power. Lean on and depend on that Intelligence.

People who contribute to the world do not find a cave and hide themselves in that cave. They let their light shine in the midst of humanity. They make the world a better place in which to live. They let the power, the strength, the courage and the intelligence within them come forth and change things.

Gather yourself together today. You are a total person. Feel the oneness of your being. You lack nothing. You are living in totality because one Mind, one Power, one Principle created you.

Say to yourself:
I look to those things in my life which need healing and program my subconscious mind to react in a healthful, wholesome way. I do a thorough job of reconditioning my thinking so I will not backslide into old habit patterns. I am equipped with all I need in order to handle everything

128

I meet in life. I stand strong and steadfast in the realization that I am a total individual, made of the substance of life and endowed with the powers and potentials of life. I live fully and freely, and contribute to my world. I know I am equipped with all that is necessary for a successful, prosperous, happy, loving life. Under all conditions, in all situations, I draw directly from the infinite Source and experience peace and strength, and the knowledge that I am in command of my life.

The Power of Thought

When we come into a true understanding of the power of thought, we make wise choices that expand our experience of life. Limitation is a state of mind and yet it is very real to the one experiencing it. Know today that Universal Law does not know limitation. It is infinite, yet it does not even know itself as infinite. It knows only to act upon the direction given it.

The limitation you experience, you place upon yourself. It is self-imposed. If you believe you are limited, you will experience limitation. You are constantly addressing your subconscious mind whether you are aware of it or not.

What a wonderful thing it would be if, in our early years of academic training, we learned that life is limitless and that limitation comes by way of ourselves. This knowledge would open many areas that otherwise remain closed to us and would help us tap the resources within ourselves.

Your true nature is limitless and the more you can move into that consciousness, the more abundance there will be in your life. You are the one who sets Universal Law in motion. It is receptive but impersonal and the opinion you have of yourself will automatically be acted upon by this Law. Your life cannot change until you change your opinion of yourself.

What the entire human race believes and accepts is exactly what Universal Law acts upon. What the world is going through right now is a consensus of the opinions and beliefs of a majority of the people of the world. We will have peace in the world when more people desire it. Universal Law will bring it about.

Do not look upon yourself as an average person, because you are not average. This viewpoint is not egotistical. You are not claiming for yourself anything that is not true of others, but if others want to feel they are average, they will live an average life. If you feel you are above average, you will experience a higher grade of living. The way is open to all.

Sometimes we look upon those who have made the greatest contributions to humankind as oddballs. They seem different from others. That is because they have not seen themselves as average. They have dared to see themselves in a larger framework. You can cease to see yourself as average and thus call forth the greater potentialities lying dormant within yourself. As a divine idea, you can express at the highest level you can conceive.

Jesus, Moses, Krishna, Gautama Buddha, and many others had the ability to see in terms of the Universal, to see beyond the small self, to take all within the scope of their consciousness. It is important that you get this universal idea about yourself, rather than the usual limited concept.

When you think of yourself as universal, do not see yourself as a carbon copy of anybody else. You do not have to imitate. You do not have to fall into the same pattern as the other fellow. You recognize that you are an original idea from an originating Mind.

There is nothing which will kill the creativity within you

more quickly than trying to be like someone else. That does not mean you oppose others. It means that you recognize you are not just another face in the crowd. You are you. You are unique. You are a divine creation of Infinite Mind. When you realize this, you will set aside the idea of a little self and widen your horizon.

Most of us restrict our livingness. If we would but look at the pattern of our lives, we would find that most of our thinking is done in a circular manner and within the framework of what has been thought throughout the ages. Let us begin to break the mental chains that bind us and think in universal terms. Say to yourself often, "I am the universal Mind in action. I open my consciousness to a greater awareness and I experience a greater depth of the beingness that is within me."

It does not matter what role or roles you are playing in life. You may be an executive, a housewife, a salesman or a laborer. The need is not so much to work toward making a new impression outwardly, but to make a new impression on Universal Law. To do this, you must have a new impression of yourself. Then life acts this impression out.

I will give you a very simple illustration. One day I watched my children making cookies, the kind you take out of a package and slice. They wanted a design on them so they took a fork and pressed on the tops of the unbaked cookies. You are doing the same thing in your life daily. Ask yourself, "What kind of impression am I making on life?" Universal Law will duplicate the impression you give it and return it to you. It cannot give you anything different. If you feel that life has dealt with you erroneously or cruelly, look to yourself and find out what impressions you are making. Ask yourself, "What is my mental attitude? What impression am I giving my subconscious mind regarding my future? What impression am I giving my subconscious mind regarding my finances, my health, my happiness?"

Universal Law operates at the level of the impression that we make upon it. If there is anything in our experience that is not to our liking, we must begin to make new impressions. Many of us have been living counterfeit lives without realizing it. We have lived by the thoughts of others. We have depended upon things and occurrences. We have blamed all our misfortunes on everything except ourselves.

Say to yourself today:

I want good to enter my life. I want health to be my experience. I am expecting opportunities to reveal themselves to me. I impress upon my subconscious mind exactly that which I want it to express through me. I look for new ideas to impress upon it daily.

As you do this, realize that you are not just changing words. You are literally changing your position in relation to Universal Law. You are changing your position mentally, emotionally, physically, and spiritually. This change is necessary for something different to happen. If you were playing chess or checkers and saw the winning moves necessary but did not make these moves, you would not win the game. The same is true in life. It is not enough to see that changes must be made to win; you must actually make these changes—and where are these changes made? In consciousness. Change your position in consciousness and then all the outer conditions of your life will change also.

Many times individuals come to me and say, "I am looking for a new job." What they need to look for first is a new consciousness. Whatever the need appears to be in our lives, no matter what form it takes, what we need is to reposition ourselves in mind first.

Say to yourself today, "I am repositioning myself right

now. My whole mental attitude is changing. I am making a new impression on my subconscious mind, one of abundance, and I see this abundance expressing in all departments of my life."

As you reposition yourself in consciousness, you will find that your ideas about finances change. You will begin to see that you *can* instead of *can't* afford. You will see that you can afford to be healthy. You can afford to be happy. You can afford to experience all of the good things in life. I believe that when Jesus said, "Take up your bed and walk," he was in effect saying, "Reposition yourself in consciousness. Move into a new aliveness of life."

Remove the Pebble

Sometimes we do a good job of sabotaging ourselves when there is no reason for doing so. When you feel inadequate, you are throwing sand on the wheels of your inner machinery. You need to cease depreciating yourself and begin to appreciate yourself. You need to realize that infinite strength and divine power are within you. You have to know that you have not been shortchanged by life. Life is always giving, but you must accept.

Say to yourself today:

I am going to start right now to heal the hurts within me. I refuse to hurt. I am going to heal the hurts by removing them from my consciousness. I forgive myself. I release myself from guilt feelings, anxiety, tension and fear. I have a healthy, robust opinion of myself. I have a true sense of worth.

This is what I call "seeing the light." Spirit in you is light. When you know the truth about yourself, you let your light shine. You can only experience you, so know yourself as you truly are and in so doing you will experience the best in your life.

Often we are unaware that we are denying our own good, our own prosperity, our own happiness. Haven't you seen people on the brink of a wonderful experience who cave in and acquiesce when something happens to prevent it. What is inside that individual that does not want to experience something good? Is he punishing himself? Does she feel that she is unworthy? Are they afraid? Whatever it is, they are denying their own good.

If your good always seems just out of reach, sit down and ask yourself what it is within you that is withholding your good. Do not try to think or analyze. Let the question sink into your subconscious mind. Ask yourself, "What is inside of me that is denying me my good? What is inside of me that is causing me to hurt?" Then listen for an answer. You will get the answer by way of a strong impression, a feeling or an idea.

Do not be afraid to ask. Be honest with yourself and you will find out what is preventing you from experiencing what you should be experiencing. You are not a victim of misfortune. You and I both know that we are products of our own thinking.

We are the beneficiaries of our own consciousness. There is only one governing Power and it governs by an exact law. "As ye sow, so shall ye reap." Get into this realization. Say, "There is one governing Power and I am going to hold fast to that which governs, for its government is always for my good."

No matter what you have let govern your life up to now, you can transcend it by deciding what shall govern your life from this moment on. Everything which has been uncomfortable and has governed your life up to now suddenly becomes secondary when you begin to operate from the one self-governing Power, the one Intelligence, the one Law and the one Principle. When you make primary in your consciousness that which has, in truth, been primary all the time, then you are being governed by First Cause.

Say to yourself right now: "There is only one infinite, divine, perfect, governing Power and that Power is in me, of me, as me, and for me right now." Hold fast to this thought. Give it supremacy. You are not sweeping problems under the rug; you are taking command of your own life. Let everything else be subservient to the one governing Power. Everything!

The intelligence within you is more than automatic. It has the power of selectivity, the power of choice. You can choose what you will in your life and you can name it what you will. Why? Because you are, in a sense, your own father and your own mother. You birth and rebirth yourself in consciousness throughout, not only this lifetime, but all eternity. You are not fragile and finite. You are the individual of all time and eternity. You are a divine inspiration and manifestation of infinite life and love.

What more can you ask for? Probably only a deeper and deeper realization of what is true, a deeper realization of the perfect pattern within you. It was through seeing this perfect pattern that Jesus could do the work he came here to do. He set the perfect example and when we can do as he did and realize and accept the Christ within us, we will no longer have to walk by faith. We will have perfect sight, perfect knowing.

Realize that "I am that I am" and the power of that "I am" is your power also. It takes effort to convert your consciousness and turn in a new direction, but the effort is infinitely worthwhile. Life is a growing, unfolding process. Embrace the Truth and grow in beauty and compassion today and every day.

Say to yourself:

I am unlimited in my spiritual power. Right now, this moment, I relate to the perfect pattern, the Christ conscious-

ness within me. I increase in love, in wisdom, and in strength. I am now in harmony with all that I do and undertake, for perfect love makes everything clear and beautiful to me.

Chapter Eight

~~~

Belief
Determines
Experience

We are chemists in the laboratory of the Infinite. What then shall we produce?

—Ernest Holmes

~~~

There are only two ways to live your life. One is as though nothing is a miracle. The other is as though everything is a miracle.

—Albert Einstein

Prayer is not for the purpose of making things happen, but rather to provide within ourselves an avenue through which the events and conditions we wish to experience can happen.

What we change when we pray is our own consciousness. We change our attitude; we change our feeling; we change our image; we change our thoughts. Prayer is that activity of our consciousness which clears out the debris, the confusion, the fear, and the negation from our thinking so we can focus on Truth. Prayer is for the purpose of changing our own consciousness, not another person, place or thing.

Effective prayer does not involve using will power. There is no forcing. There is knowing. It is not something we do to another person but rather something we do to ourselves. If we pray for another person, we do not "send" that person anything; we do not hold in our mind anything for that person. Prayer is something we do within ourselves, regarding that person.

Through prayer you know the Truth and when you know

the Truth, it sets you free. What is the Truth? The Truth is that there is only one Mind and whatever is known in universal Mind in one place is known instantaneously in all places. You do not have to know the name of the person for whom you are praying. All you have to know is that Mind, which is universal, which is everywhere present, knows that person; therefore, you can know the Truth about that person right where you are and establish an avenue through which positive change can occur in his or her life. Truth is universal and being universal it knows no time or space.

Prayer is an action of the mind of the person who is thinking right thoughts. You do not go outside of your own mind to produce a healing, whether it be mental, physical or emotional. In prayer there should be a realization and an awareness in you regarding the spiritual perfection of the other person.

No matter how imperfect the world looks or how impossible a situation seems, there is a seed of perfection within it.

Begin your prayer with the realization that the seed of perfection is there and that you are dealing with a principle that works absolutely and perfectly.

When you become aware of this inner perfection and are totally convinced of it, then take definite and deliberate action to remove every thought from your consciousness that would obstruct or prevent this perfection from appearing. If what you are praying for is abundance and you seem to be caught up in lack, it is your *belief* in lack which needs to be erased so abundance may be made manifest. Know that the seed of abundance is within you. Accept that seed of abundance in you. Be certain you are not thinking thoughts that will create an obstruction. Prayer precipitates the removal of the obstruction of thought so that the flow of perfection may be made manifest.

Prayer is not the use of autosuggestion. It is the realization of Truth. Do not try to convince yourself that all is well in the world of appearances, but that appearances can be changed by changing your consciousness to a realization of Truth.

Do not work with appearances, but work with the Truth. You are not changing the effect, you are working with the cause. Get back to First Cause.

Prayer is the neutralizing factor which enables you to look at an appearance and to be still and know that there is perfection back of the ugly appearance, that there is nothing wrong with the seed of perfection and that it will blossom. You never heal a condition. What you heal is your belief about the condition. Your belief is the only thing which needs to be healed, regardless of what the condition is. You do not fight the condition, the situation or the surroundings. You know the Truth. Resistance to evil gives it life and power. When it has no life or power it evaporates. If you work with the conditions, you are working with effect. By knowing the truth, you are working with the cause. This does not mean that you put a blindfold over your eyes. What it means is that the change must take place in you.

Thought erases thought and thought replaces thought. Prayer is the art of keeping your thought focused on the perfection of your being. Our world is created by our consciousness. It is important to realize that the very Law which binds us is the very Law which frees us. We do not have to fight and struggle but we do need to know the Truth. Truth alone sets us free. Infinite Intelligence knows nothing except perfection; Mind does not know lack of any nature. This is why you can work on your consciousness and know that you are working on the solution to your problem. Stop working on the problem and start working on the solution. Remember, the solution already exists in Mind.

141

Say to yourself right now:

Today I give no power to the world of appearances. I center myself in the Truth and I see the perfection of life in me and the perfect working of the law taking place all around me. I align my thought with the living, loving Presence.

The Law of Belief

What is your belief about yourself? What is your belief about life? It is important for you to know, for Universal Law works according to your belief.

You are affected—either positively or negatively—by your beliefs. The Law has nothing to work with except your beliefs. We might say that Universal Law is your belief in action. Each person is living life at the level of his or her mental acceptance and according to his or her beliefs.

When you change your beliefs, you change the law of your life, because you change your consciousness. We read in the Bible, "I can do all things through Christ who strengtheneth me." Why? Because your Christ Consciousness is the spiritual wisdom within you. It is the power which moves into activity according to your faith and your belief.

In the Science of Mind, we teach that you can do all things through the Christ Consciousness within you. You can call this inner power by any name which suits you, but whatever name you give it, it is there within you ready to go into action for you.

Belief begins as a thought which you accept. You cannot buy beliefs in a supermarket. You "manufacture" them in your consciousness. Sometimes when you examine your beliefs, you will wonder when and how you came to believe that way. In fact, until you pin your beliefs down, you are not always aware of what they are and how you are affected by them. This is why it pays to know what you believe.

Since belief is a mental conviction, let us decide today that we do not believe in lack, in harm, in being hurt, or in loss. We believe in life. We believe in health. Whatever appearances we meet to the contrary, we need to stand firm in our beliefs. If all of us believed constructively, there would be no sickness, no harm, no lack, and no crime. We must keep our own consciousness clear, for anything that we believe in, we give power to.

When you do not believe in these negative things, there will be nothing in you to bring them into your experience. Through the law of attraction, you attract to you according to your own belief. Begin to probe yourself in relation to your beliefs. What do you really believe? Are your beliefs destructive or constructive?

Today, change the direction of your thoughts and your beliefs, and keep them changed. As you do this you will change your destiny, for you make your destiny with your beliefs.

Imagination

If you want success, you must be able to envision it. If you want health, you must be able to envision health. If you go into business with a vision that the business is going to fail, what will happen? It will fail, of course! Whatever you want, then, you must be able to envision in consciousness. You must be able to let the imagination play upon it and make it as vivid in your mind as possible.

You must have a vision, and the more conviction it carries with it, the more powerful it is, the more powerful the subconscious mind will be. Universal Law will attract to you that which you envision. You build the concept with your imagination and the Law builds the form. It is no different than furnishing an apartment or a house. You furnish it first in your imagination and then you purchase the items you need to make your mental image a reality.

Look at life the same way. Life is meant to be a beautiful experience. How do you furnish it? With what kind of thoughts do you furnish it? With what kinds of ideas do you furnish it? You have consciousness within you and the imagination to see life any way you would like to see it. It is up to you.

No matter what adverse circumstances or hardships we may encounter, by the right use of the imagination, we can get ourselves out of any predicament. By using our imagination to work in harmony with Life, we are working with Truth. The results have to be favorable.

All of us must use our thoughts and imagination in our lives. Many of us are not careful about what we allow ourselves to think. In our idle moments, we let our imagination run wild.

It would be very enlightening if each of us had a tiny tape recorder with us everywhere we went and this recorder automatically turned on with every negative thought we had. Later, we would be amazed to play the tape back and hear some of the idle thoughts we had indulged in without consciously thinking about them. It pays to be aware of what you are thinking. Your thoughts can kill or cure you.

Say to yourself right now:

I use my imagination in a constructive manner. I do not let myself indulge in idle, negative thinking. I let any hurts that come to me act as stepping stones to a higher good. I know life is always blessing me and that by the right use of my imagination I can create a better tomorrow.

Receiving Your Good

Today, open your mind. Open it completely. Come into a new and open consciousness.

A beautiful life and a beautiful world await you, but you can only experience them when you are willing to see them from a new standpoint, the standpoint of Truth and not of appearances. Today, get the feeling of receiving. Get the feeling of life pouring itself through you. Say to yourself right now, "I am receiving new ideas. Spirit is pouring itself through me. I am receiving creativity, health, wisdom and guidance."

You do not have to reach out in every direction for inspiration. You can look within and know, "I am receiving beautiful ideas. I am receiving health. I am receiving joy. I am receiving my good. I am receiving my answers."

Get the receiving feeling, for that is the Spirit pouring itself through you. As long as you are looking, you are not receiving. As long as you are looking, you have not found. As long as you say, "When will my good come to me?" just so long are you deferring your good. You are not receiving. You are not accepting.

We sometimes spend a lifetime seeking that which we already have. We give power to effects and not to Spirit. Jesus never gave power to effects. I am not saying that you should deny that there are certain appearances in your life, but I am saying, "Do not give them power. Do not fight them. Do not sweep them under a rug. Do not wrestle with them at all. Look at them, but in consciousness strip them of all power."

I believe the secret of Jesus was that he gave all power to Spirit. The appearance was there. Fine. But Spirit, Mind, Life, Intelligence was the power. Let the Infinite pour through you in the same manner. Receive it. Accept it. Know that it is the only power in your life. Say to yourself right now:

I am letting the infinite Power express itself through me. I am
receiving my good.

If you can do that for a week, wonders will happen in your life. You will receive your good. You will feel the Spirit pouring through you. There is no power outside of you that can act upon you. Grasp this point today.

The appearance might be there. I do not deny that, but there is nothing outside yourself which can affect you. There is nothing outside of yourself which can destroy, harm or take good away from you.

If you remember that there is a Spirit within you that is all-wise and all-loving, if you remember that this Spirit created you and dwells within you always and that it is love and intelligence and truth, then you know that appearances have no power. We experience according to our beliefs. If you give dominion only to Spirit, nothing can harm you in any way.

Today, let the best in life happen to you. Let Spirit within you be that which impels you to action. Let the Truth take over in your life. Let the Power within you be the only power you acknowledge. Look at appearances and give them no authority to move you. Look at them, but know the Truth. If you give them no power, if you do not feed them in any way, they will evaporate.

You can be constantly emerging from old concepts into new ones if you are open and receptive. You can constantly see yourself in a process of becoming. Just to think about wonderful things happening to you is not enough, though. You must know that they are now yours.

Happiness Is Now

You are the sole cause of your world. No one else can be the cause of your world.

If you find yourself in situations you do not like, you are there because of your own consciousness. To change your situation, you must change the direction of your thought.

It is said that energy follows thought. Is your thought going in the direction you want your energy to go? If not, face about in consciousness and reposition yourself. Others may try to discipline you, but this type of discipline is of no value until you sit down and begin to discipline your own emotions, your habits, your time and your thoughts. When you do this, your energies will go in the direction of your good—that is, along constructive, creative and productive avenues.

Life wants us to be happy. If I am miserable that is my own fault, because life itself is basically a dance of joyous creativity. Even though this is true, I can look the whole world over and not find happiness until I sit down and know that I *am* life, I *am* love, I *am* happiness. Everything I want must proceed from within my own consciousness. There is only one Life and that Life is infinite, but within that great Life everything that exists, lives and moves and has its being. That Life is your life right now. You live and move and have your being in Life, which is Intelligence. Life wants you to be happy. It wants you to express the happiness that is within you. Stop seeking. "Be still and know."

Isn't it wonderful that there is Something in this universe which wants you to be happy? It doesn't have to make you happy, because you are already created of happiness, but you can only experience that happiness at the level of your own understanding and at the level of your own acceptance.

The gift has already been made. You do not have to seek

it. You do not have to earn it. It has been given. You have the freedom to accept this gift or reject it. You have the freedom to create, the freedom to perform, the freedom to pick yourself up and do what you want to do. In other words, you have the freedom to direct your own life.

Once you make up your mind what you want to be and to do, you begin to realize that as soon as you came to this decision, you set Universal Law in motion to fulfill it. Everything is done first in consciousness and then experienced in the outer world.

Through prayer you can change your life by changing your thoughts. Prayer helps you to keep your thinking directed along constructive lines. It helps you to build firmly in consciousness. Consider a contractor, for example. He must take the plans drawn by the architect and carry them out in the minutest detail from the foundation to the finished building. If he thinks something would be better another way, he must consult the architect. He does not change it on his own.

The same is true of Universal Law. It takes the plan you give it and works it out just as it is. But you, being the architect, can change the plans at any point you wish. If you want something different and better in your life than you envisioned at the time of conceiving and drawing the original plans, do not hesitate to change them according to your desire. The Law will, then, automatically change its way of working them out.

As the designer of your life you have a right to change it at any point, for your life is not made of concrete but of living substance. Who of us is wise enough to see our whole life in minute detail just as we would want it? At different stages of unfoldment, we think we know what our entire life should be, but another enlightenment comes and we see better ways of doing and being. And we should be ready and willing to change accordingly.

Say to yourself today:

I am the designer of my own life. I was created to be free and happy. I was created to express the creativity within me. I entertain only thoughts that will bring me a richer, happier, better way of life, for I am the one who decides. I am the one who chooses in which direction my consciousness shall go. I change my mind and I keep it changed.

Satisfaction and Accomplishment

Find the place you are to fill in life and then fill it to the best of your ability. Do not try to be something you are not but do whatever you do well. Naturally, you want to constantly improve and expand. You want to feel a sense of satisfaction and a sense of accomplishment.

There is a miracle Power working through you and this power knows no limitation or stopping place. It does not hurry. It does not push and shove, but keeps constantly and steadily surging forward, opening worlds before it and leaving worlds behind it. The Infinite ever entices us and draws us onward to discover more.

Whether you fully understand this miracle Power or not, you can know enough about it to enrich your life in every way. You can prove to yourself that this Power works by means of you. Remind yourself often of this Power. Know that it is within you and all around you. Know that it is constantly healing and blessing you. Know that it is leading you toward greater satisfaction and accomplishment. Through consciously using this Power you can change your life. You can let go of that which is hindering you and impress your subconscious mind with that which you desire.

It is always hard to realize that you are the cause of your

own suffering, yet with this realization comes the understanding that if you are the cause of your suffering, you can also create your good. The mental process that creates what you experience is within you. It is not outside of you. Nothing can happen on the outside until it begins to happen within you.

There is only one Power and that Power is within you. That Power operates through faith and belief. You have to have faith in yourself. You have to have faith in Universal Law. You have to have faith that you can create new avenues for living. You can heal your body. You can heal your thought. You can heal a situation. You can heal a condition, and the way you heal any of these things is by a process of faith.

Yes, this healing Power is right within you today. Know that, and know that you are always demonstrating your beliefs. When you believe in the perfection of your own being and put your subconscious mind to work for you and not against you, you will be more satisfied with your life and you will accomplish more.

Everything appearing in your world corresponds to your beliefs. You create your world by means of your beliefs, so enlarge your faith, enlarge your awareness and enlarge your beliefs. If you are not experiencing what you would like to experience and if you are not satisfied with what you are accomplishing, you can change your direction.

This Power within you is not something you can half believe in. It is something you must trust wholly. You must rely upon it totally. You must know that Universal Law is operating for you and through you. It operates for everyone. If this Power appears to operate more readily through one individual than another, it is because that individual trusts the Power more than another.

How strong is your belief when you pray? Do you expect

results, or do you merely hope? Do you expect to experience the good you desire, or do you merely wish? What do you expect today as you go about your business of living? Do you expect the best or the worst? Do you expect problems or do you expect solutions?

There is no reason in the world why you should not live a happy, satisfying life filled with one accomplishment after another. No, there is no reason in the world. If you are not living this kind of life, then the reason is within you. You can look within yourself and find the reason and change it. The miracle power within you is always ready and willing to take new and better directions. This is the only way it can release its riches to you. All you need to do to set it in motion is to have the right consciousness and give the Power an opportunity to prove itself to you.

Few people can dramatically change their lives overnight. It takes a great deal of culling out of the old and replacement by the new. It takes a great deal of constructive thinking and an abiding faith, but what others have done, you can do also.

There is no limitation to what you can accomplish. You will expand and accomplish throughout eternity. You will grow and grow and grow some more. There is no reason why you should be a doormat today. There is no reason why you should not take every opportunity today and live it to the fullest, to experience it in as great a depth and height as possible.

Say to yourself right now:

I am never content to remain in one place in consciousness long, for I know there are worlds and worlds in consciousness to become aware of. I choose to savor life as I live it. I accomplish what I can each day and pave the way for more accomplishment tomorrow. I experience a great satisfaction in life because I do not put off the living of it today.

Realize that you have a place in life to fill that no one else can fill, for no one else is exactly like you. No one else can experience life exactly as you do. No one can fill the niche that is yours to fill. Realize, also, that you can fill this niche to the fullest by trusting in the Power within you. Open yourself to this Power today and know what it is like to experience a satisfying life filled with greater and greater accomplishments.

Say:

I look upon life as a wonderful opportunity to grow and expand. Satisfaction is mine today, because I am accomplishing according to the divine pattern within me.

Chapter Nine

~~~

Opening
to the Infinite

I do not know what I may appear to the world, but to myself I seem to have been only a boy playing on the seashore, whilst the great ocean of truth lay all undiscovered before me.

—Sir Isaac Newton

~~~

We are never left without a witness of the Eternal, and in our greatest moments—in those flash-like visions of mystic grandeur— we know that we are made of eternal stuff, fashioned after a Divine Pattern.

—Ernest Holmes

Your conscious mind is the doorway to your creative center. We live in a world where there is much negativity, and we must let the conscious mind stand guard at the door where thoughts of every nature seek entry. It should be selective. It should evaluate that which it takes unto itself.

Your subconscious mind looks for the conscious mind to give it impressions and directions. You are always impressing the subjective side of your being. When you hear, see or touch, it is your conscious mind that is seeing, hearing and touching. It is your conscious mind which analyzes. It is your conscious mind which makes the selection. Your subconscious mind does not select. It acts upon the impressions given it.

What you ask of your subconscious mind, it will do for you. If you need it to gather together and reveal data to you, it will do so, for whatever you need is in this subjective storehouse. It will do what you request, but it will not volunteer its services.

You might think of your conscious mind as a swinging

door which opens in two directions. It swings open to the outer world and swings in to your inner world, permitting both input and output. Many thoughts slip through without being consciously chosen. They are like children who romp into the house with dirty feet before their parents are aware of what they are doing.

This is why the conscious mind needs to stand guard at this swinging door. We must be aware of what we are letting in and what we are calling forth, for when we give the subconscious mind the right impressions, we experience the right expressions.

The subconscious mind is intelligent. It performs perfectly if it is not given cross-purpose directions. For example, it knows how to regulate the body. It knows how to properly circulate, assimilate and eliminate. You do not have to know these things consciously. It can fulfill any creative activity you choose. If you are wounded, it knows how to mend the wound. It knows how to coagulate the blood, so if you are cut you will not bleed to death. It knows how to breathe in and out. All of these and many more things, the subconscious does automatically.

However, there are other things which can only be acted upon by the subconscious if it is given some sort of impression or direction. The conscious mind must come into play when we wish to change our habit patterns, in the case of both actions and mental/emotional responses. The subconscious part of us is subjective, or subservient, to a higher command—the command of our conscious thought. The conscious mind blazes trails. The subconscious is there to "stand under" and support what the conscious mind does.

The moment Spirit enters into a new human conception, the subconscious begins to build the body. The child in the womb is automatically taken care of. It cannot say at this stage, "I am I." It may have an oceanic feeling of oneness and a sense of belonging to the All, but it does not consciously know what the All is. The conscious mind has not at this stage taken over. Even after birth, the subconscious carries on with the building and growth of the body.

Say to yourself right now:

I am a thinking, choosing individual. There is a power-house of creativity and intelligence within me that knows what to do, how to do it and when to do it, but I must consciously choose that which I want it to act upon.

As you stand guard at the door of thought today, do not feel you have to suppress anything to keep it from manifesting. Suppression and repression are a holding back, and like steam in a kettle, that which is suppressed or repressed will push its way out. Am I saying that if you are angry with someone you should lash out? No, but do not grit your teeth and let the anger go underground either. Sit down quietly and ask yourself why you are angry at that person. Get to the heart of the matter.

Are you acting immaturely? Are you reacting to old thoughts and feelings? Have you simply failed to stand guard at the gate of thought? You can usually find the reason and clear it out of your consciousness without resorting to action you may later regret.

Take thought today as to what you entertain in your conscious mind, for it will be subconsciously acted upon.

Say:

I identify with the greater Intelligence within me so I may think and act with wisdom. I am aware of what I let enter the door of my consciousness.

Stop Seeking

Spirit is everywhere and you are an embodiment of it. Begin to realize the rich dimensions of yourself that can unfold. When you feel isolated or cut off, that is because in consciousness, you are not in tune with the Infinite. Life is a continual process and you are a part of this process.

You are never without a light to guide you, and this light is within you. You are the light of your world. As you turn within, become aware of the light within your own consciousness and let this light reflect out into your world.

You were not put here to grope around in the darkness. Groping, suffering and darkness are created by negative imaginings. Life is love and you are here to express the love and light that are within you. When you realize this truth, your daily life will take on a whole new dimension of livingness.

You have many choices open to you. You can choose a corner and you can sit in that corner and do nothing. You can search far afield for a sense of identity and purpose. Or you can realize what you are and begin to express it. Within you is a continuous flow of creativity. It was not intended that you be ongoingly static or idle. You were not created that way.

Every part and particle of you is active. Every atom within you is dancing the dance of life, though to the outer eye at any particular moment you may appear anything but active. Ideas are always flowing within you. Wholeness is always present. Abundance is always at hand. But until you become aware of this and act upon it, it does not manifest in your life.

You are constantly bursting with new, creative energies which are eager to radiate out in all directions, encompassing your world. Think of yourself today as bursting from within, touching new dimensions of consciousness, facing new experiences, realizing new ideals. Life only becomes stale to us when our vision is focused downward or when we take the world of appearances at face value. Look inward and radiate outward.

Say to yourself today:

I am the center of my universe and my universe is centered in me. No one can experience for me that which I can experience for myself, nor can I experience for another. I am open and receptive to life today.

All Life lies within us and before us, but we must do the taking for ourselves. The spiritual kingdom is here on earth. It already exists in its completeness, but we must recognize that and partake of it. If our life seems a total void today, we need to make the choice for it to be otherwise, determining that we will experience all the joy of living and the fulfillment that life has to offer.

Stop trying to change the world "out there." Stop trying to change people "out there." Stop fighting situations and circumstances. Get to the center of your being and find the reality of life itself. Every cell you have within you is part of a divine design. It does not come into being by accident. Every cell bursts with the allness and fullness of life. Individual cells change, but the life process goes on.

Life is a continuous process, a process with many changes. If we tried to hold on to old cells which had served their purpose, new ones would never have a chance. The same is true when we cling to that in our experience which should be released. The newness awaits us, but we must let go of the old and make room for that newness.

Do not be afraid to let the past go. You can be assured that if you let it go, something more desirable will emerge, for life is a continuous process of betterment and carries you into higher and higher dimensions of awareness.

What if the cells in your body said, "We like it here and we are going to stay here"? What would happen to the body? Every cell is born, fulfills its divine intent, and then moves out at the end of its cycle, permitting new cells to come forth.

Say to yourself:

I am a cell of life. I am a cell of the universe, of the entire universe. I am here fulfilling a divine design and letting the divine intent within me ever unfold. I am not afraid to let go of that which is completed and finished in my life in order for something greater to take its place. I am always open to realizing new and expanding dimensions of consciousness. I let go of one cycle of living for a newer and better one. I do not hold on.

There are cycles within cycles within cycles in the unfoldment of life, but the people who insist on remaining right where they are do not realize that they are the cause of their own suffering. They refuse to change and unfold. I am not denying that change can be painful, but the pain will be nominal if we change willingly and do not become set and fixed in our old ways of thinking. Anything is easier if we can flow with it instead of fighting and resisting.

Somewhere along the path, we dull our senses; we dull our creativity; we dull our spontaneous expression of life. Why? Is it because we have been hurt? Is it because we are afraid of loss or pain? Or is it because we are too focused on the world of appearances to look within and see the real world, the world that can give meaning, purpose and fulfillment to our lives?

The only place you will find meaning for living is within your own consciousness. The only thing that will give meaning to your individual life is the meaning you find within yourself. Only your recognition that you *are* Life and that you are here to give expression to that Life will enable you to fulfill your divine destiny.

Today, stop seeking and start realizing that the heights and dimensions of life are within you and ever await your expression.

Say:

I am a fountain of Life. Newness is constantly flowing through my experience. Change is constantly taking place. I do not have to seek for what I already am. I do not have to look for that which I already have. I flow with the continuous process of life.

Living from the Center

When fear steps in, your faith is limited. When negation takes over, you cannot see the truth. Anxiety is failure to remember that you are greater than any situation or any condition, and you *are* greater, much greater, than you know.

Work with yourself in consciousness. You do not have to grope and fumble through life. To know that you are one with Divine Power is not egotistical. It is to know the truth about yourself—that life, power and consciousness are within you.

Say to yourself right now:

If infinite Mind is one, and it is all in all, then Divine Intelligence is the sovereign power in my life. If I am what Spirit is, I cannot be less. I have only to see this truth with singleness of vision in order to rule over my life.

The higher self within you has the power to rule over all worldly elements in your life. It has the power to rule over fears, conditions, situations, and it has the power to direct your life in ways of peace, plenty and beauty.

What a wonderful feeling you will experience when you realize that all you must really develop is consciousness and that within your consciousness you are king or queen. You are the ruler. You are the governor. The knowledge gives you a great sense of freedom and power to be and to do what you really are.

Why don't we experience what we truly are? I believe it is because we look outward instead of inward; we focus on the false instead of the true. As long as we see falsely and accept illusion for truth, we will continue to experience less than our complete good.

Have you ever felt snubbed? Didn't you feel hurt about it? Have you ever had the feeling that no one understood you?

You can be sure that the individual who says he or she is never hurt is the one who is hurting the most. He just does not admit it. He is too prideful to say he is hurt. All of us have hurt feelings at one time or another, but we need to know that it is the pride and the ego that are hurting. It is not the real self.

What we must do is work on ourselves in consciousness. We suffer more from our own attitudes than from the false opinions of others. We suffer because we expect people to act in a certain way and to respond in a certain way, and then we become disappointed. Who disappointed us? Not really the other person, but our own expectations of what the other person should do or be.

You have heard people say, "My children have disappointed me. My best friend has let me down. I have been hurt by my closest relative. The people I do the most for do the least for me. When I need my friends, where are they?"

We must look within ourselves to see what triggers our hurt feelings. Of course, we all have the right to let ourselves be hurt. We have the right to decide what others should do and then be disappointed. We have the right to make such choices, but is it worth it to do these things to ourselves? I think not.

Not only do we sometimes expect too much from others, but we also expect too much of ourselves. We over-extend ourselves. We try too hard to change ourselves or to make ourselves accomplish more and more. That does not mean we should not try to improve ourselves, but sometimes we try to do it all in one big leap, when it should be more of an unfoldment process.

Expect and demand the best from life, but do not demand of yourself that you accomplish everything all at once. Expect everything that is good, wonderful, healthy and joyous, but recognize that everything in nature unfolds by degrees.

There is a time and a place for everything in your life and you do not have to push and shove, forcing and making excessive demands of yourself or others. There is always more good coming up for you tomorrow.

Develop an expectancy consciousness. Life will give you what you expect of it. This consciousness of expectancy will constantly lead you in progressive ways, and your good will unfold as you go along. All things stem from consciousness. You must *know* that there is infinite good in your world for you, or you will not experience it. Let it unfold; do not force it. Know that your good is always at hand and will be revealed to you as you go along.

Say to yourself:

I have an expectancy consciousness. Infinite Intelligence is my source. The Truth is my source. I go to the Source for manifestations of good. This Source is my help in every need. I do not have to struggle and over-extend myself. I trust, and my good unfolds as I go along in life.

Infinite Intelligence in you is your help in every need, so go directly to the Source. Anchor yourself in the Truth. Know that everything you experience is going to stem from the divine awareness within your consciousness. "...as he thinketh in his heart, so is he." You cannot experience that which you cannot

163

encompass in consciousness, but you can do all things through the Christ within you, which is the almighty Power at the center of your being. Remember, "Spirit in me is one. Beside it there is no other." If you can do this, you will not let secondary things take on too much importance in your life.

Everything you need in order to lead a joyous and fulfilling life is within you. If your opinions about yourself, life and others are limited, then you will not attract the best. If your attitudes are negative, so will be your experience.

You are not at the mercy of the world. You are not at the mercy of other people, or the government, or conditions or situations. You are at the mercy of your own consciousness. You are at the mercy of your own beliefs and your own expectations. You are at the mercy of your own attitudes.

Of course, you are not going to learn everything at one time. There will be times when you are hurt and disappointed. There will be times when you feel alone and left out. There will be times when you experience what you feel are the brunts of misfortune. There will be times when your ego takes over and pride stands in the way of the Light.

There will be these times, but you can make them less and less in your life. Just remember that all is consciousness and that nothing comes to you except by right of consciousness, whether it be for good or ill. Know that the Spirit in you is whole and when you operate from this center of oneness, nothing of lesser degree can enter in.

Say:

The good in my world is infinite. It unfolds for me in every way every day. I anchor myself in Truth, and the riches of life pour through me, making my way straight and making my life beautiful. I am fulfilled day by day.

Never Poor

Department store magnate J.C. Penney had a beautiful philosophy. He said, "You may catch me broke, but you will never catch
me poor." J. C. Penney did not have a poverty consciousness.
This is why he could be broke without being poor and could
always reestablish himself.

There is a vast difference between an individual who has
a fear of poverty and an individual who may temporarily be
broke or out of funds. The individual who is temporarily broke
will always come up with more money, but the individual who
has a poverty consciousness will never come up with anything.
Poverty will always find its way out through him.

People with a poverty consciousness will always lose money.
No matter what they touch, it will turn sour, while the individual
who has a wealth consciousness may have setbacks but will
bounce right up again.

We can relate these two types of consciousness to more
things than money. We could call them a "have" and a "have not"
consciousness or an "abundance consciousness" and a "lack
consciousness." They work in all areas of our lives in the same
manner as they do where money is concerned.

Suppose my back hurts today and tomorrow my legs ache.
The next day my shoulder hurts, but when that lets up, then my
neck or my hip gives me trouble. What is happening? I not only
have what appears to be many health problems, I have a
consciousness problem, and that is the consciousness of lack. I
feel that I lack health and this lack takes many forms. Is this not
a poverty consciousness?

When we hurt or when we fail all the time, we can trace this
condition to an initial or "parent" consciousness, which gives
birth to many children. The parent always breeds children after

its own kind. What we can do, then, is to build a new parent consciousness that will be more in line with what we want. We can build a prosperity consciousness which will parent abundance in our lives.

The basic issue we have to deal with and heal is the idea of separation from Life. To feel at one with Life is our natural state.

Say each day, "I am never separate from my good. The one Life that exists is the life that is in me and all around me. I am one with this Life." Use any other words that have meaning to you, but let this statement become a daily habit. It will help you feel your at-one-ment with all of life and help eliminate any consciousness of lack or poverty.

The greatest curse of our civilization is the feeling of being separated, isolated and alone. It makes us feel small and insignificant. It cuts us off from others. It cuts us off from our good. It separates us from our source of supply, from our health, our security, our good and our friends. It builds up fears of every description.

What happens when we develop a consciousness of abundance and realize that we live in an indivisible universe where no separation can take place, not ever, except in our own consciousness? Things begin to change. We think in terms of unity. We know there is no separation. We know the universe is unlimited and that unlimited blessings can unfold in our lives. We know our good is all around us and within us.

Whenever this realization comes to you, you will be healed of a belief in loss, but as long as you fear loss, you will experience loss. If something in your life seems to be healed and does not remain healed, it is because the parent thought pattern has not been changed.

Jesus, Buddha, Moses and many other great individuals had the right parent thought or consciousness. That is why they could give so much love and light to the world. That is why they were able to channel so much wisdom, so much beauty, so much truth. They experienced life according to the type of consciousness they had. We do the same, and if our life today is not to our liking, we can be sure we must change the consciousness that is parenting that which we do not desire to experience.

Say to yourself:

I want a whole new thought pattern from which to operate. I desire to change my lack consciousness into an abundance consciousness. I mean to change my consciousness of separation into one of unity. I know that by approaching this from the inside out, my life will take on new patterns automatically. I will not have to work on each individual problem separately, for my taking care of the parent will cause those problems to be cleared up at the same time.

You are setting up within yourself a new causation, and the resulting chain reaction will take care of the subsidiary or satellite problems. This principle is the same as the one that would operate if you said to an interior designer—and, by the way, you are the interior designer of your consciousness—"Here, take this room and redecorate it. I want it done in good taste. I want everything to fit right." A good designer would come up with something of beauty and harmony. And so can you. We experience life according to our belief, according to what we give Universal Law to work with.

We should not say, "Give me a little relief. Let me feel good for a little while. Give me a little peace. Give me a little letup from my problems." As long as we are willing to accept only a little of anything, that is what we will get. However, we can use the principles of the Science of Mind to pattern a whole new consciousness, a consciousness of oneness, of wholeness, of abundance in all things.

Dissolve your poverty consciousness and replace it with a

prosperity consciousness. Recognize the constant availability of an Infinite Intelligence and a Divine Presence, which is always close at hand. This dynamic realization of your oneness with Spirit will set your whole world right.

Infinite Intelligence, expressing as you, wants to distribute new ideas through you, abundant ideas. You are an originator. It is up to you to originate in your own manner. You must learn to do so without placing any limitations upon infinite Law, without placing limitations upon yourself. When you align yourself with the Infinite, your consciousness will cause good to be rained upon you in unlimited abundance.

The Law of Increase

There is abundant evidence all around us that the law of the universe is one of increase. All you have to do is plant one sunflower seed to get a huge sunflower and hundreds of seeds to prove this law to yourself. Everything propagates and multiplies lavishly after its own kind. There is a law of increase inherent within everything.

Those who do not know this law of increase will say to someone who is manifesting good in abundance, "How lucky you are! Every direction you turn something good happens to you." No, the individual is not "lucky." We always experience life according to how we approach it. Doors will open for us—new doors—when we open our consciousness more. The better the ideas we entertain within ourselves, the better the thoughts we think, the more we raise our expectations, the more we will experience.

To think constructively and creatively, we must reposition ourselves in mind. We turn in a positive direction. Doing so frees us to move from glory to glory—from one fulfilling level of consciousness to another, from one set of affirmative expectations to greater ones.

We must learn to use the law of increase to better our situation in life. We do the inner work first, then once our thinking is lifted up, we need to move into physical action. We do not wait for manna to fall from the heavens, for we are not wanderers in a desert without food and drink. We are manifestations of Life and have our own self-contained food and drink. We are like the seed which has the potential to become the sunflower and to propagate many seeds.

Our seeds are our thoughts and actions, our emotions and our attitudes. We can have anything we want, but we have to work for it. It will not just come. How do we work for it? In consciousness. We have to prepare our way in consciousness. This means that we must change our consciousness and keep it changed. We must free it from misconceptions and come to see and know the Truth. Only then we will be free to move ahead into a new life.

We were not born to suffer. We were born to live life lovingly, joyously and to multiply our good. Say to yourself right now:

I have been entrusted with life. I have been entrusted with
a mind. I have been entrusted with a body. I have been
entrusted with the ability to move and to speak. It is up to
me to use everything I have been entrusted with.

Begin to bless the good in your life and watch it multiply. Let your tap roots go deep into consciousness. Do not look at lack and loss. Do not depend upon luck or chance. The Spirit in you is greater than anything that can happen to you.

Rejoice today in your own good. Rejoice in the good of others. You do not have to be jealous of what other people have.

You do not have to envy them. You do not need to resent anyone. You have the power to be fruitful and multiply. You have the power right within yourself to increase your own good. Say to yourself, "Unlimited good of every nature is constantly increasing in my life."

Till the soil of your mind. Till it and plant the seeds of your desires. Plant seeds that will enrich your consciousness. Use every talent, every gift you have—and you have many, regardless of whether you are aware of them or not. Realize your spiritual inheritance. Become aware of your marvelous endowment. Increase your health. Increase your happiness. Increase your substance. Increase your opportunities. Bless what you have. Share what you have.

Enter today into an awareness—a keen awareness—of the law of increase and what it can do for your life. Remember, though, that it works like a double-edged sword. It can multiply your good or it can multiply your ills. What it does depends upon where you position yourself in consciousness.

Say:

I prepare the soil in mind, plant the right seed and reap a bountiful harvest of good in my life today. I know Infinite Intelligence and I are one.

Chapter Ten

~~~

Change, Chaos, and Transformation

One must have chaos in oneself in order to give birth to a dancing star.

—Nietzche

~~~

In my end is my beginning.

—T. S. Eliot

~~~

In my Father's house are many mansions: if it were not so, I would have told you.

—John 14:2

*L*ooking out upon the world today, we know we are living in rapidly changing times. We are living in a new day and age, and we witness swift transitions all around us. We see the birth of newness and innovation taking place before our eyes.

We witness—but this is not enough. We must be part of the action. We must adjust and adapt. This means we must have a consciousness which is able to be open and receptive to change. We cannot allow our consciousness to dwell in the old tents of tradition or depend upon ways of the past. This would amount to putting new wine in old bottles and the essence of today would be lost.

Today demands fresh and original thinking of each of us. We must keep abreast, in consciousness, of all the activity and change going on about us. We must release oldness for newness. We must look ahead, not behind.

Today, the vision of science is giving us new modes of transportation and new avenues of communication. It is making changes in every area of life. It is unfolding new fields of electronics, medicine, psychology and even religion—new ways of looking at the truths which have come to us down through the ages, ways that bring more peace and joy and livingness into our lives.

With our ideas about the universe changing, we must change our religious concepts, envision anew our relationship to life. A new scale of values is needed. Life ever demands adjustment to change. The expression of life must be kept flexible and fluid. When we experience conflict within ourselves, we can be sure that we have allowed ourselves to become crystallized and stationary when, instead, we should be moving ahead with this newness all about us.

Life, inwardly and outwardly, is urging each of us: change, change, change! Move out of old ideas and concepts. Feel the fire and the surge of newness taking place all around you.

Scientists have learned to split the atom and release nuclear energy. What an awesome and wondrous achievement! How shall we use this energy today and in the tomorrows to come? Will we use it for the destruction or for the betterment of humanity?

Immediately, we are faced with the necessity of goodwill. Goodwill is in the realm of moral values and moral values are in the realm of religion. So we find that religion must be practical. It must be ever-alive and fresh in the present, something that can be put to practical use in our everyday living.

Jesus, the Teacher, when he brought forth a new frontier of thinking, did not lean on the morals of the past, but stood on nowness. He said he came to fulfill the law—fulfill, not destroy it—but he fulfilled it in the light of his day's needs, not the needs of the past. This is what our religion must do for us. It must be current with the times to meet the needs of the times.

The Science of Mind helps keep us abreast of today by teaching us how we will always be able to meet the tensions and problems in our lives. There will never be a time when all tensions cease, all conflicts subside and all demands are met. The fact that we have experiences means that we will meet with tensions and demands and conflicts. *How* we meet them depends upon our internal resources. The Science of Mind teaches us how to draw upon our inner resources, to handle with equanimity and grace the turmoil of everyday living.

Ask yourself a few pertinent questions: What kinds of things upset you the most? How do you use your religion in handling them? Does it facilitate self-mastery and poise? If something has been upsetting you for the past three, five or ten years, you are probably not using your religion to its fullest. How, for instance, do you react when someone hurts your feelings? Do you erupt in anger? Do you snap back? Do you brood?

Let us go a little further. What are you afraid of? What within you is dividing your house of consciousness against itself? What are you doing to yourself? Why are you allowing fear to sour your consciousness and ruin your happiness?

All fearful conditions and situations can be handled through the aid of the Science of Mind philosophy. Philosophy and religion are for the purpose of teaching us to handle problems victoriously. A mind which defeats itself before it confronts a problem is already defeated. But the mind that is alert, awake and alive in the face of a problem, that thinks only in terms of a victorious outcome, will surely see triumph.

Let us joyfully acknowledge a Divine Power that is in us, working through us. Divine Mind is an Infinite Presence of love and law, not a deity who says, "You've suffered long enough, now I will reward you." The Spirit within you says, "When you look unto me, there I am. When you open your heart, you will find me. When your consciousness is receptive, you will receive your good."

Let us promise ourselves today to get out of our prison of false thinking. Let us climb out of the prison of limitation and with profound faith walk away from our fears and doubts, and know that there is an invisible Power which will honor us. Let us move now into the timelessness of life and feel the glory of a joyful Beingness creating through us.

All of this can come about by our willingness to flow with life and our willingness to change. This is a new age. We cannot stop with the prophets of the past, but we can bring the past up to the present and expand it into newness. Prove Universal Law to yourself in the spiritual laboratory of your own mind!

Let us blaze new trails, taking with us the divine idea that we are at all times using the mind of Infinite Perfection and forever are we immersed in the living presence of Universal Spirit.

Disenchantment

There is not a single one of us who has not been disenchanted at some time in our life. Perhaps a love did not turn out as we idealized it, or a job lost its glamour for us. Were we not the ones to glamorize and idealize in the first place? Were we not the ones to coat the situation with illusions of our own making instead of seeing things as they really are?

If we are not seeing truly, we cannot experience truly. Disenchantment gives us an opportunity to correct our vision and see things in a more realistic light. It gives us an opportunity to move forward.

Sometimes disenchantment comes from trying to hold

ourselves and others to the same thoughts and the same feelings that have always existed. This is a mistake, for no moment is ever the same. Life is fluid and constantly moving and our concepts of it and of individuals should change as time goes on. Do not feel guilty if you cannot think and feel just as you did yesterday. Rejoice that life offers you new exhilaration and excitement as you grow.

To grow without being constantly disenchanted you must discipline your thoughts, feelings and attitudes. This takes effort and it takes time, because it is a program which requires the making of new habit patterns and keeping those habit patterns uppermost in mind and heart.

Most of us do not want to take the time, make the effort and give the attention to a new life pattern. This is why we so often muddle around instead of getting somewhere in consciousness. We want a little genie to come and perform for us. When nothing happens because of our halfhearted attempts, we say, "See, nothing changed. I knew it would not work!"

We must remember that it took a lot of thinking to get us where we are today and it will take a lot of thinking to move us forward to greater experiences. Say to yourself, "Thought by thought I got myself into this pool of negativity. Thought by thought I will get myself out of it." And you will, but it takes discipline.

Discipline is simply the act of keeping the mind and the emotions aimed in the direction you want them to go and not letting them return to old directions, old habit patterns. This takes a great deal of affirmative prayer and meditation. It takes a constant attuning of ourselves to the Infinite.

You can't pretend the problem doesn't exist and make it go away. Let's take a garden, for example. If you went into your garden and saw weeds there, would they go away if you said,

"They are not there"? Of course, they wouldn't. You would have to uproot them and pull them out. You might change the chemistry of the soil so they could no longer thrive. It would be ridiculous to expect them to remove themselves. If you want to use the ground for a better purpose, you have to make some changes.

The same is true with the weeds in our minds. If we do not want them there, we must do something about them. To pretend they are not there is just kidding ourselves. We must clear the soil of mind, prepare it for what we desire and plant new thoughts there. Then we must nurture these thoughts with positive expectations and faith until they grow into a new awareness, a new realization.

Jesus said, "...I, if I be lifted up...will draw all men unto me." If the Christ Consciousness within us is lifted up, we will draw our good to us. Work thought by thought with your consciousness until you become aware of the Divine Presence that is within you. Affirm the Truth until it becomes true to you.

The word *affirm* means to declare or state. Whatever you affirm in your mind long enough and strongly enough will manifest as an experience. Therefore, if you want to change your life and express more of the creativity within you, stop affirming what you do not want and begin affirming what you do want.

Your life is not like an object you place on the mantel and look at now and then. You are not here to collect dust in some obscure place. You are an expressive part of life.

Life is vital and alive, and I say to you that if you have always wanted to do something, start it. If there is something you have always wanted to tackle, tackle it. If there is a hobby you have always wanted to enjoy, begin it today.

Do not say that you haven't time. Take time. You do not

have to wait until the day when time just comes along. The time is now. Do you really want to do it? If so, then start it. The only time you can express your creativity is now. The only time you can bring newness into your life is now.

When people are engaged to be married, they have a light in their eyes. They are excited. They are filled with anticipation. Get the idea today that you are engaged to this thing called life. Fall in love with life. Life itself will never disenchant you, nor will your love of life be a disappointment to you. There will be a new expectancy arising within you each day. You will feel the wonder and beauty of life. You will thrill to it. You will know how marvelous it is to be alive.

Does a person in love want to go and sit in a corner and gather dust? No. Neither does the individual who is in love with life. That person wants to participate. That person wants to experience fully the joy of living. If you have experienced aches and pains, aggravation, disappointments and letdowns, turn away from these disenchantments and discover and uncover within yourself that which will liberate you and bring you a new life.

A Little Bit of Jonah and Job

Often we are closed-minded. We all know people—like Jonah in the Old Testament—who refuse to be changed one iota. They will listen to you but not permit you to make a dent in their mental armor.

As long as we try to live life with preconceived ideas and set opinions, as long as we are inflexible, we are trying to live with a Jonah consciousness. The writer of this Bible story was trying to tell us that we must become more flexible and that we must

179

be open to new ideas. We create our own hell when we become rigid and leave no room for change.

There is no greater feeling of release and joy than to be able to say "I have been wrong" and turn in the other direction. Jonah would rather have died than to admit he was wrong. Many people would rather suffer than give in. This is what Jonah was doing when he went through the feeling of a psychological death. This is the meaning of his being in the dark belly of the whale for three days and nights.

This is a most beautiful story, but a symbolic one. It deals with the subconscious. The story is trying to tell us that we create our own hell by being so set in our ways, by being so rigid that we cannot see and admit our mistakes and thus go on to something better.

We must be big enough to admit that we are sometimes wrong, that we sometimes make mistakes. We do not have to make a big production of this. We do not have to dwell on the mistakes, but until we can see our mistakes and admit them, at least to ourselves, we are not free to release them and accept new ideas and new ways.

If you find yourself in an unforgiving state of mind, ask yourself, "Why am I doing this?" Probably you are hurting; probably you are set in your opinions; and just maybe you are feeling sorry for yourself. When Jonah came to his senses, when he realized what he was doing to himself, he was cast upon dry land. He was not thrown again into the ocean to be swallowed up by another big fish and thus dwell in darkness again. He came to a new understanding. He had something solid from which to operate.

The whole story is telling us that we must be able to look at negative conditions and say, "Despite all the ills that I thought were before me, I know there is a better way. It is great to know

I can change." Jonah did not change until he had crucified himself and dwelt in the tomb for three days. This is what being in the belly of the big fish for three days means. It is an Old Testament version of what happened to Jesus in the New Testament. After three days in the tomb, Jesus arose; after three days, Jonah was cast upon dry land.

Let us go from Jonah to the story of Job. We often hear, "He has the patience of Job." Job did not have patience. Job means "persecuted," and who persecuted Job? Job persecuted himself, until he was restored to his senses. There was a battle going on in Job as there is a battle going on in each of us. We all have a little Job in us. We persecute ourselves constantly and we do this until we arrive at a point where we are restored to our senses.

Job, in spite of his wrestling with himself, never completely lost his faith. He clung to a thread of Truth. Trials and tribulations, illness and everything imaginable happened to Job in his consciousness. At one point he realized what he was doing to himself and said, "For the thing which I greatly feared is come upon me, and that which I was afraid of is come unto me."

Yet this realization did not bring him to his senses at that time. He suffered more. Finally, we are told that Job repented in sackcloth and ashes. He quit wrestling with himself. He came to his senses. He was restored to his right consciousness.

"So the Lord blessed the latter end of [Job's life] more than his beginning." He had new riches, more children, a beautiful life and lived to a ripe old age.

In the story of Jonah, we see rigidity, stubbornness and unforgiveness. In the story of Job, we see a very negative disposition, wrestling with all its negations, until he realizes he cannot win by fighting that which is bothering him, though there is something which can bring him out of his misery.

181

Sometimes we are Jonah and sometimes we are Job. We bring what we fear upon us. We struggle with things until we see a better way.

Say to yourself:

I am willing to admit when I am wrong, so I can release what's no longer useful and be free to move into that which is more joyful and fulfilling for me. I quit wrestling with the negatives in my life. I put my trust in the Infinite. I am infinitely blessed.

Life does not pick on us. We bring our confusion into the household of our own consciousness, but there is the Infinite Knower within us which can bring us back into balance. If we but let go of the clamor of hearsay and of opinions and listen to the still, small voice within us, we will know that.

The Second Birth

You cannot be in two places at once and neither can your thoughts. If you want a different experience, then you must turn your thoughts in a different direction. You must awaken to what you want and then take a stand, let go of the old and take on the new, release the lesser and grab hold of the greater.

Until you convert your thoughts from illness to health, you will not experience wholeness. Until you convert your thoughts of lack to those of abundance, you will not experience plenty. Until you convert your thoughts of unhappiness and misery into thoughts of happiness and joy, you will not experience abiding peace. This change, this conversion, this right-about-face must take place within your own mind and your own heart.

Your life will not change until you attain and maintain a new attitude of mind. No one can give that to you. When you, yourself, begin to accept, declare and feel that a new experience of life is yours, it will come to pass. As Job said, "Thou shalt also decree a thing, and it shall be established unto thee." You have to know what you want and then decree it—speak a word. When you accept it subconsciously, your ideal will come to pass. This process is important to understand. Your subconscious mind is always on the job and its job is to bring to pass that which you have decreed and established in your consciousness.

We interfere constantly with our own good. Life is always presenting opportunities for us to follow that will take us forward, but we often negate them. As long as we think in a negative manner, we will experience life in that same manner. We are destructively using the same principle that we could be using constructively.

Every area of your life should show definite signs of increase, definite signs of improvement and advancement. Why? Because that is how life works—because the mind cannot stand still, and you are mind, and mind is constantly expanding.

Since you are mind and mind is constantly expanding, then the subconscious mind within you is also forever expanding. You interfere with this expansion if you put negative patterns into the subconscious. You restrict your own experiences.

The subconscious is a builder and it will build, but it can only build what you give it. If you give it a negative pattern, it can only build on that basis. You can begin to say right now, "This is the end of negation." You can begin to feed the subconscious mind with right ideas, ideas that are enriching in every manner.

Thoughts of jealousy, thoughts of anxiety and any kind of envy tear down and destroy us emotionally, mentally and physically. Jealousy is one of the most destructive weapons we can use against ourselves. It blinds us to our good and when we indulge in it, we no longer think clearly, creatively or lovingly.

Let us realize that it is self-destructive to be jealous of anyone. Jealousy can only exist by feeding on a sense of ineffectiveness and powerlessness. Jealousy indicates we are experiencing a sense of lack and insecurity. In a way we are reprimanding ourselves for not having done what we ourselves feel we should have done.

Whether we like it or not, each of us is where we are by right of consciousness. When we change our consciousness, our lives will change. Jealousy, envy and resentment will not bring to us what we desire. If we are not experiencing what we would like to experience, then we must look within ourselves and examine our focus and commitment.

Ask yourself today, "Am I jealous of another's good? Do I envy what another has? Do I resent it because another has more than I?" If the answer is yes to any of these questions, look within yourself and find the beliefs which restrict you from creating for yourself a similar experience. We are never jealous when we know, as did Abram in the Old Testament, that all we can see, we can have.

Change your thoughts; change your feelings; change your ideas about having and having not. Say to yourself right now:

> I am a divine idea immersed in Infinite Mind. I do not
> envy anyone, because I have the same mind that everyone
> uses. I am not jealous of anyone, because I know we each
> have what we have by right of consciousness. I do not resent
> anyone, for I know that resentment poisons me. I am
> capable of doing and being and having the same as any
> other person. Today, I turn my thoughts and my feelings
> in a new direction. I cast out all negativity of every kind.
> I dwell on those things which will enrich and enlarge my

life. As I take a new direction in consciousness, my outer life also takes on a new direction.

Begin today to think and plan for yourself. Do not let yourself be blinded by appearances. Know that the subconscious mind is the builder in your life and that it will build according to the blueprint you give it.

The Rhythm of Life

The ancient Hindu scriptures teach that life is a dance, and I believe they're right. You must get into the rhythm of that dance, of life. You must feel the pulse beat of life, the flow of life, the breathing in and out of life. Physically, the earth expresses these rhythms with its seasons, its periods of night and day, its tides. Each thing which exists must fit its rhythm to the beat of life. Each must find its own place in the dance.

Only you can sense this rhythm for yourself and react to it in your own individual way. When all the rhythms are blended together, they express as a great symphony.

Why not decide that you want to be doing something special and enjoyable, listening to the beat and rhythm of life, feeling the pulse of it? Say to yourself, and let it sink into your consciousness, "Life is a dance. I move with this dance and know the beauty and rhythm of life. Life to me is joy. Life to me is happiness."

The principle taught by the Science of Mind will aid you in putting a bounce and rhythm into your life. This principle is based on the premise, "As you believe, so you receive," and it suggests a way for you to *change* your beliefs by beginning to think new thoughts. Therefore, re-condition your mind. Say, "There is an infinite intelligence, an infinite Mind and I am one with that Mind. There is one infinite Love, one infinite Life and one infinite Truth, and I am one with this oneness."

You must enhance your recognition of this oneness. You must know that everything you undertake is part of the One. There is really no human mind, no human negation, no human fear; but rather, one infinite Intelligence, one infinite Life which is divine. What, then, divides you? You divide yourself in consciousness and you must reunite with the unity of the spirit of your being. You must arrive at the consciousness of knowing the truth of this unity.

Spiritual understanding will give you a new realization. It will bring you into a new awareness. You can go home and you can look at the same people, you can have the same business, do the same work, and yet with this new realization and understanding, all will appear transformed. You will not only see everyone differently, but you will feel differently toward them. Always, as you get new concepts about life and new ideas about yourself, everything else changes for the better.

Right where you are, mind is. Right where you are, life is. Right where you are, love is, and so are peace, plenty, wholeness and beauty. So is the rhythm of Life itself. If you would feel the dance of life within you, you have but to attune yourself to this rhythm.

Today, ask yourself, "What false claims have I allowed to attach themselves to me?" Do you have a false idea about your health, your wealth, your relationships? Erase these from your mind. In reality, there has never been a sick body. There has never been a sick mind. There has never been a sick business. There has never been a sick life. But we have had sick beliefs about all of these things.

Ernest Holmes, the founder of the Science of Mind philosophy, once said to me, "There is nothing to heal." This was difficult for me to understand. There was much evidence to the contrary. But I pondered his statement many times in the days to come, until I finally understood that indeed there is nothing to heal...except my thoughts and beliefs.

I believe we wrestle too hard to heal this and that. We forget that Something within us which is "closer than breathing, closer than hands and feet." We forget that within Spirit "we live, and move, and have our being." There is no outside. There is no separation, except that which we permit in our own consciousness. When we realize this, life does, indeed, become a dance of joyous acceptance.

In Psalm 100, we read these words, "Make a joyful noise unto the Lord, all ye lands. Serve the Lord with gladness: come before his presence with singing. Know ye that the Lord he is God: it is he that hath made us, and not we ourselves; we are his people, and the sheep of his pasture. Enter into his gates with thanksgiving and into his courts with praise: be thankful unto him, and bless his name. For the Lord is good; his mercy is everlasting; and his truth endureth to all generations."

Doesn't that give you an uplifted feeling and make you want to sing and dance with thanksgiving that you are who you are and that all life, truth and beauty are yours for the accepting? You have freedom of thought and freedom of action, but you must realize and accept this freedom. Not even Spirit can give us that which we will not accept, but when we get into the feeling of oneness with all life, we no longer wonder that life has been depicted as a dance of joy.

Maybe today you feel that your life is crumbling to bits, but where are you looking? Are you looking outside at appearances, or are you looking within? Look within and you will find much to be thankful for, much to be happy about, much to praise and appreciate.

Say to yourself right now:

I praise the life that is within me. I praise the life that I am within. I appreciate the freedom that is mine. I am filled with the wonder and beauty of life. I get into the rhythm and the swing of it. I know the joy of oneness. I am in step with life and move to its rhythms with grace and ease.

Living is a joyous experience when you get into the rhythm of it. I do not mean that you have to go around singing "joy, joy, joy" with every breath. Simply know that you are born out of joy and that joy dwells deep at the center of your being.

When you think of Reality, think of that which is uplifting. Think of that which gives you peace and comfort. Think of that which sings and dances within you. Then let your whole being sing and dance with it.

Say:

My heart sings and dances with the joy of being alive, of being in a universe that is always giving of itself and that embraces all of its creatures with love and tenderness.

Chapter Eleven

~~~

Make Your Dreams a Reality

The future is made of the same stuff as the present.

—Simone Weil

～～～

The minute you begin to do what you want to do, it's really a different kind of life.

—Buckminster Fuller

～～～

I have a dream.

—Martin Luther King, Jr.

～～～

More things are wrought by prayer than this world dreams of.
—Alfred, Lord Tennyson

You and I have a great power within us, for we have the ability to think and to manifest what we think. To set this power into motion in the direction we want it to go, we cannot just wish or daydream or be idly ambitious. We must have a strong desire and then subjectify this desire. We must know that Infinite Intelligence is expressing itself by means of us.

Hope will not get the job done either. It takes applied faith to accomplish your desire. It takes using the creativity of your mind and the play of your imagination, and it takes stick-ability. You have all of these qualities within you, but they lie dormant until you put them to use.

When we become still and turn within to make contact with That which can bring all things to pass, doors will begin to open for us. Ernest Holmes said, "That which you are seeking is seeking you." The experience you are seeking is already waiting for you. It wants to manifest by means of you. Be still and know. Be still and become aware that you do not have to go anywhere or do anything in order to make this contact...other than to be open in consciousness.

Faith and desire will unlock the power within you. You do not want to just talk about it or hear about it. You want to experience it. You want the dynamic ideas it contains to flow through you into expression. You do not want to unlock this power in another. You want to release it within yourself. You want the benefit of its wisdom to be channeled through you.

Jesus told us that faith can work miracles. Have we, after two thousand years, taken this statement to heart? If we had, what we look upon as miracles would have been taking place in our lives daily as a natural result of our faith.

What a magnificent consciousness Jesus had! This is why his results were so great. If we could but attain this same state of consciousness, we would not have to go around begging for half a loaf when a whole one is already at hand.

This idea reminds me that many people followed Jesus to obtain "loaves and fishes." Only a few sought that inner strength and power which made his demonstrations possible. Do we not do the same? We should be aware of that and let our results become secondary. First, we need to establish the right con-sciousness and then all things will be added unto us.

No matter how many possessions you have, your life will be empty until you touch and experience the infinite Intelli-gence within you. The only thing which limits this power is you, yourself. You must unlock the door of inner consciousness in your eternal search to know more about this thing called Life. I am sure there are many, many inner doors of consciousness which open upon greater and greater vistas of livingness, but the only one you can open at this time is the one that is before you. Once it is opened, others will present themselves.

You set your own pace, fast or slow, but what you must do

first is *to begin*. The Power is so vast and so great that it can release you from all forms of tension and fear, doubt and anxiety, uncertainty and confusion.

Know for yourself today, "I am this living Power. I am experiencing this Power." You will bring this Power through you in your own unique and individual way. There is no set way. There is no one way. You must find your own way to tap this Power.

Successful people are only successful because they recognize and admit this Power, by whatever name they call it. You can be sure that anyone you greatly respect, anyone you look upon as a great individual, has, in his or her own way, tapped into it.

Say to yourself:

I am the Power. I am this infinite Power.

Remember that a successful, creative individual helps make the lives of others more complete. If you are healthy, happy and prosperous, using the Power within you, you are an example to your fellow men and women. You are an inspiration for them to go and do likewise.

That Power is impersonal and universal, though you make it personal to you in the way you use it. In most modern buildings, there are many electrical switches which control certain operations, but there is one called the master switch. If the master switch is on, everything else will operate. If it is off, nothing will work. Similarly, in ourselves, there is a master switch in consciousness, and it comes on when we recognize our connection with the Infinite.

Within each of us there is a switch for truth; there is a switch for knowledge; there is a switch for beauty. In fact, there is a switch for everything, but the master switch must be on for others to operate. This is why it is so important for us to become conscious of the Universal Mind, the All-Knowing Mind, the master switch, the spiritual "power button" of consciousness within us.

Say to yourself:

The Power is within me. As I take mastery over my thinking, I align with my highest good. This intangible power becomes tangible by means of me. Though I cannot see it with my physical eyes or touch it with my physical hands, it is the reality of my being. I let it be the master switch which, turned on, sends the dynamic life force to my body, my mind and my emotions. I live with grace and ease.

There is something within you that causes you to think, to move, to act, and that something is the universal Intelligence within you. Like the air you breathe, it is unseen, but it is the source of everything you do. You do not have to go looking for it on top of a mountain. You do not have to get it from a guru. It is within you. It has always been within you—because you are the Power.

Say:

The power within me is spiritual Power. It is the very precious gift of life to me. I make my contact with this Power, and my burdens become easy and my load becomes light.

Master-Minding

Mind is capable of all things when we do not use it simply as a means of coping with our outer world. It is not just something to think thoughts with. It is much more than that. It goes beyond words and thoughts into the realm of creativity.

Think of yourself today as using the Master Mind, or

illuminated consciousness, not just the surface of the mind. Jesus used the Christ Mind and this same mind is within you. Begin to use it today. Say, "I am master-minding an ideal. I am master-minding a new, dynamic expression of life. I am master-minding my whole life."

This means that you are accessing the unlimited Power within you. Realizing the supreme Power within, you feel and know you are in command. You are master of all situations. You know you can use the omnipotent energy of this Master Mind which is within you. You do not have to depend solely upon the objective, thinking, analyzing, figuring side of mind. You can go to the Knower within.

Naturally, the objective side of the mind is important, but it is only important from the standpoint that it carries out what the Master Mind has given it. When we plant seeds in the subconscious side of the mind, we expect Universal Law to work on them according to the nature of the seed. When we master-mind something, the seeds themselves come from a higher Intelligence, which makes no mistakes.

This does not mean that you cannot take these seed ideas which come from the Master Mind and, with the objective side of the mind, plant them into the subconscious side. It means only that you do not depend upon the objective side of the mind, with its human limitations, to *produce* seeds. Seed ideas which come from the Master Mind are potent and perfect for growth in your consciousness and in your life.

When you employ the Master Mind, you are employing the Knower. You are employing the infinite side of life. You no longer feel helpless or hopeless or uncertain. You know you have the ability to handle yourself and to handle all situations.

This is a marvelous feeling, this feeling of being in command, of having the power of the whole universe back of you.

You begin to think in terms of master-minding everything that pertains to your life. You know that the Knower within can master your thoughts and meet every challenge. As you practice master-minding, you produce the mastering quality in your life.

You develop leadership qualities. You will consistently take command over yourself. This means you will have command over what you think. You will direct your emotions in support of your ideals. You are going to realize that you are the master over your body. You are going to take responsibility for your own life and not lean on others. You can experience this mastery when you know that the mind that was in Moses, Buddha and Jesus is within you also, and that it will operate for you as you let it.

When we say we have a conscious mind, a subconscious mind and a superconscious mind, we are speaking only of the uses to which we put Infinite Mind, the level at which we are using that Mind. Most of us use the objective level and we should be able to figure everything from that level. This is not true, for its boundaries are limited and within its boundaries we are simply hashing over the old.

We need to delve deeper into the realms of awareness to live our lives from a higher level of spiritual enlightenment. We must learn to master-mind ourselves. It is always ourselves that we are master-minding, never anyone else. We are mastering our own thoughts, our own feelings, our own actions, and we do this by letting the Master Mind lead the way.

Many thousands of people have used this Master Mind throughout the ages. They called it by various names, but all of them were drawing upon the Power within. Moses, Jesus, Krishna and Buddha are outstanding examples. You, yourself, use it when you turn within and seek guidance and enlightenment.

Too many people are merely trying to cope, to tolerate

things. They make themselves ill. They will continue to do so until they come to the realization that there is no need to cope any longer. There is no need to tolerate any longer. There is no need to endure any longer. When they realize this truth, they come into an entirely new expression of life. They begin to master-mind themselves. Self-mastery is the only mastery we need, for from that all our growth and good will flow.

It does us no good to have money if we don't spend it for things we need. It does us no good to have this master-minding power within us if we never use it. So, think of yourself as being a successful man, a successful woman, a successful business person, a successful mother or father. Give the subconscious mind an image of success. At the same time let the Master Mind pour forth into your consciousness those ideas that make for success. You will find that your business increases. You will know better health. You will experience more joy and happiness in your life. You will be on better terms with all you meet.

The benefits above are the "added" things that come from seeking first the kingdom of heaven, or the Master Mind within. Consciousness comes first. Realization of the inner power comes first. The feeling and knowing of the kingdom of heaven comes first and then all else is added unto you.

As you become master of your own life, you will find that you have mastery over your circumstances. All you have to do is take command of your life and let the Master Mind within you empower the action.

Say:

I take command of my life today by turning to the Master Mind within and letting it initiate dynamic leadership in my life. Thus I am master of myself and of my world.

The Success Consciousness

Suppose you are reading a book which is considered a best-seller. Did it become a best-seller because the author sat down and typed out a rough draft and sent it in? No. First, he had to get the idea, then he had to plan the way he would work the idea out, and then came a rough draft. After this there was considerable editing and revision before it was typeset. Even after that, it had to be proofread again for mistakes before being sent to the printer.

Talk to any author who has written a best-seller. Say to him, "You have hit it." "Yes," he will say, "but also let me show you a box full of rejection slips that came before it was accepted!" It isn't that he is counting all the rejections and moaning over the manuscripts that came back. He is simply pointing out that it took time, energy and effort to reach the best-seller stage.

Some writers who become successful say that before they were famous, they could paper a room with their rejection slips. Most of them admit they learned a great deal from them. First, they learned what the publishers did not want; second, they gleaned much valuable help from the criticism that came back with the rejections.

Some would-be writers never become authors because they quit trying to write after receiving their first rejection slip. They consider themselves failures, inadequate, or they feel that the publisher cannot see how good their work really is. Whatever their reason—or excuse—for quitting before really trying, they are not willing to take a realistic look at themselves and their work to see where they can learn the successful way of accomplishing it.

If an artist gave up because nobody bought his or her first picture, if an engineer or architect walked away because his first plans were not accepted, how would any of them ever know what they were capable of doing?

Sometimes we walk away from life. Life is exciting, but its excitement is also challenging. It requires something of us. It requires the use of all of our talents and abilities. It offers opportunities, but these opportunities must be realized by effort on our part. They are part of our overall growth and we cannot grow and develop without putting forth energy.

Today, do not look at your competitors. Look at yourself. What do you want to accomplish? In what do you want to succeed? Decide and then direct your energies toward accomplishment. Those who have made great contributions to life have had to believe in the principle of creativity within themselves, and this is what each of us must do in our own way.

Do you remember when you were small that every year you would back up against the doorframe and be measured? What a joy it was to see yourself grow half an inch or an inch, or maybe even more! I know there were many notches on the doorframe where we were measured in my childhood home.

This was physical growing. Now, I would like you to experiment with some spiritual growing. Back up to the doorframe of your consciousness and measure yourself. Are there any areas in which you would like to grow? Find one, two, three or maybe half a dozen. Write them on a slip of paper and tape them to the doorframe of consciousness, one above the other.

See how you can grow to reach these qualities you have chosen to work on. Maybe one will be health, another peace, another love, or finances. Say to yourself, "If I can measure my physical growth on the doorframe of the house, I can measure my spiritual growth on the doorframe of my consciousness. If I can grow physically, I can grow spiritually. I will fulfill my life and grow in these areas I have chosen. All of life exists to back me up."

Let this project be between you and yourself only. I know there are many things you want to experience in your life. Work in your own mind to know you have that something within you that will enable you to grow tall in consciousness. Say to yourself, "The more I think I can do, the more I can do." Do not let anyone discourage you. Do not let appearances get in the way.

All is consciousness and what you accomplish in consciousness moves out and demonstrates itself in your world of appearances. You alone can choose your rate of growth and the areas in which you will grow. But remember to persist. "If at first you don't succeed, try, try again."

Yes, try, try again. Do not let rejection slips deter you. Learn something from each experience that does not come out right. Look upon mistakes as a chance to learn and grow. Reach for the opportunities and say, "Life, I am ready now. Let's go!

Get into the consciousness today that Infinite Mind is guiding, guarding and protecting you. If your aim is high and you do not waver, you will outdo yourself and come out on top. Maintain a high state of consciousness every step of the way, knowing you can do what you desire because you *think* and *know* you can, and because the infinite Presence is there to guide you.

Say:

The more I believe I can, the more I can. I am sustained
and maintained every step of the way. No matter how often
I must try again, I do not become discouraged. I learn from
my experience and move ahead again.

As You Will

You—and all of us—need objectives, causes, and purposes for living. Without dreams and ambitions, you would have nothing to propel you forward. Life would lose its excitement and interest. Never give up your dreams. So, never give up your ambitions. Never let life get stale for you. Feel the elation of life. Do not take counsel with your fears and do not come down with your doubts. Remain forever elated and eager so you may find the true joy of life.

Even though life might knock the wind out of you for a moment, take a deep breath, brush yourself off and continue on. Where would any of us be today if, the first time the wind was knocked out of us, we allowed ourselves to feel defeated? Thank goodness there is the propulsion of Life itself that urges us on and on, that urges us to try, try again.

The beauty in the flight of a graceful bird is that it moves. It does not stay put. The same is true of a beautiful sunset, or white, fleecy clouds scurrying before the wind. Music has to flow and so do love and laughter. We must learn to extract from them the essence of beauty and delight as they happen and not try to hold on to them.

Each moment should be a moment of fulfillment. Each moment should hold its own contentment. Each moment should be a moment in which we feel the joy and the ecstasy of the indwelling Presence. Say to yourself, "I enjoy the sunset as it happens. I enjoy the flight of birds as they pass by. I enjoy the well-being of life that is within me right now. I am tender and kind today and I do not wait for tomorrow."

We limit ourselves in many areas. If we feel small and insignificant, it is not because the infinite Presence within us has ceased to be omniscient, omnipotent and omnipresent, but because we are seeing ourselves in the wrong light.

No one ever needs to feel small. No one ever needs to feel limited. No one ever needs to feel inadequate. These are only ideas with which we have associated ourselves. If I feel inadequate and insignificant, it is because I am looking at myself and I am not looking from the center out. I am not seeing on the grand scale what the Infinite would have me see. I am focused on the small self.

An individual who sees only his or her weaknesses is self-centered, but the individual who builds from the center out says, "Here I am and I see the grandeur of Life. I see the intelligence of Mind. I see the life of Spirit."

When we see only our inadequacies, we have lost sight of the divine nature which is within us. Try if you can to count all the stars in the universe. Try if you can to count every grain of sand on a beach. Try if you can to count every raindrop or every snowflake that falls. Of course you cannot. It can't be done. Here the universe is trying to tell us: "There is no limit anywhere. There is no limit in your capacity to love. There is no limit in your capacity to perform. There is no limit making you remain right where you are. All you have to do is come into the consciousness and the realization that this day, well-lived, is a day that all the beauty and life of the uplifting Power within you."

Stop grounding yourself. Take wing and begin to experience the divine nature of your being. Yes, you will travel an unknown highway that will be new and strange to you, but remember, it is not travelled alone. It is charted for you each step of the way by a higher intelligence than your own. Even if with your physical eyes you cannot always see the way, there is the Knower within you that always knows what to do, when to do it and how to do it.

What a beautiful realization it is to know that each step is under the guidance and divine protection of this Knower within. Today, live your life with a spirit of love, peace and joy. You alone can live your life, so come alive! Come alive with joy! Come alive with eagerness! Come alive with love!

Think of life as a grand feast that is always spread before you. You can partake of that which suits your nature best. The next time you feel sad, the next time you feel discontented, the next time you feel mean, the next time you feel unkind, remember: you are upset and dissatisfied with no one but yourself. The hostility and the sadness are within you. It is done unto you according to your state of consciousness. Hell is a state of mind and so is heaven. It is done unto you as you will it.

One of the greatest blessings that we have is the spirit of inner freedom — the freedom to move in any direction we desire. We can think as we will, we can believe as we will, and we can act as we will. The way in which we use this inner freedom is up to us. It is this power of freedom and choice that gets us into all of our troubles and the same power that releases us from them.

Today, take responsibility for your own life. Have the courage to live it to the best of your ability. Move with the ongoing tide. Do not take life for granted. Do not take others for granted. Do not take yourself for granted.

Have the courage to think along new lines, to express new views, to be true to the Self that is within you.

You cannot be yourself when you let the world of appearances mold you. You cannot be yourself and also always be a good fellow and go along with the crowd. You must flow with the pulse of upliftment and self-expression and think your own thoughts. If you are doing this and living from the center out, you cannot be false to anyone else. You will not hurt anyone else or limit their self-expression in any way.

Life never says, "Everything is coming up roses." It does say, "I have made you of my own substance. I have implanted within you every quality I have. I have given you infinite life, love and intelligence, but in order for you to grow and expand, you must constantly become more and more aware of this. As you do, you will experience life as it was meant to be. Your problems will become challenges that will lead you to greater progress. You will not ask for static ease but for dynamic action. You will be eager for the opportunities that carry you forward in your dreams and ambitions."

Yes, life is always lived at an individual level, not on a group or mass level. Each of us has all the power we need to be successful in our undertakings. We have all we need to create healthy, happy lives, but we must know that we are marked to win and we must then have the courage and faith to move out and make our dreams come true.

Say to yourself:

Today, I team up with Spirit. With Spirit as my partner,
I cannot fail. I cannot fall short of the mark of my high
calling. I am marked to win.

What is it you feel you need? What is it you want to experience? What is it you want to be? Whatever the answers are to these questions, know right now that the whole universe, with all of its wisdom and intelligence, with all of its love and with all of its beauty is within you. You have the courage, you have the faith, you have the power within you to accomplish. Use the gift of freedom and choice within you and know that Spirit will sustain you all the way.

Trusting Life

The subconscious mind is ready, when you call, to go into action and produce that which you desire.

Today, we often say we are calling upon the Higher Self. Jesus called it the Father within. Krishna and Buddha had other ways of expressing it, but all great teachers have felt that "something" we call the indwelling Presence. You can call it God, the Father, the Presence, or whatever name you are comfortable with. Whatever you call it, it awaits your awareness of it.

If you have faith even the size of a tiny mustard seed, you can be sure that, by whatever name you call it, it will respond to you. Say to yourself right now, "There is something in me that knows wholeness and knows how to produce it. There is something within me that knows peace of mind and can help me experience it. There is something within me that will guide and direct me, that will inspire and lift me." This "something" can give you tranquility. It can give you greater understanding and compassion.

Edison said that he did not invent but that his inventions came through him. When Mozart was asked how he composed such beautiful music, he said, "I just write down what I am hearing." One of the world's greatest engineers said that whenever he had a problem, he never lost sleep over it. He turned it over to the Greater Mind, to that Greater Self, and by morning, or sometime the next day, he knew the answer. This same Greater Mind or Self is within each of us.

Today if there is a problem for which you feel there is no solution, turn it over to this Inner Self. Through the activity of the subconscious mind, it will be taken care of. Back away from the problem. Give yourself a little room for perspective. Turn it over to the Greater Self in perfect faith and confidence that the solution will be revealed to you.

I am sure that Mozart did not write those great masterpieces in one sitting. It was done through time. Likewise, what you need will come to you through time. Have the faith of a child. Trust implicitly. Tap that level of consciousness which is always ready with the answers. If you have been carrying a problem around, just ease it off and say, "I am turning this over to the higher Self. I know the intelligence within me knows the solution."

I like to work on the idea of not denying that a problem exists but of laying it aside and saying to myself, "I am interested only in the solution. I put the problem behind me. I am facing the solution." As long as I live with the problem, it creates stress in my life and I cannot see the solution, but when I begin to look for the solution, something creative happens. Doors begin to open before me.

The process will work for you also, but you have to trust it. You have to rely upon the creativity within you. So often in this world we do not trust other people. We do not trust the government. We do not trust what is going on about us. So we must learn what we *can* trust. Back of all people, all governments and activities lies the infinite omnipotent, omniscient Life Force. As we place our trust in this Power, right action will come forth. Say to yourself now:

I trust myself. I trust Life. I know my trust is validated.

I like to feel that the Infinite sets up a trust for each of us. When we have this feeling of being perpetually cared for, we know the truth of the words of the prophet who said, "Before they call, I will answer." We know the answer awaits us, that we have but to listen and accept. It may sometimes come to us in strange ways—that is, ways that seem strange to us—but if we have the trust, we will understand the answer as wise.

Those who believe they will always be provided for will be provided for. The Power works in many wondrous and mysterious ways.

Say:

I am perpetually loved and cared for by the Infinite. I place complete trust in the givingness of Infinite Mind. I accept the changes in my life as action for betterment. My ongoingness is assured.

Chapter Twelve

~~~

Good Is Always Available

All know that the drop merges into the ocean but few know that the ocean merges into the drop.

—Kabir

~~~

Earth's crammed with Heaven, and every common bush afire with God.

—Elizabeth Barrett Browning

Opportunity is knocking everywhere, but we must open the door of life in order for life to flow, fulfilling every need.

Have you seen the very interesting picture painted by Holman Hunt of Jesus knocking at the door? Once a man who was looking at the picture turned to the artist and said, "A magnificent work of art, but didn't you forget something?" The artist looked at the picture and said, "What could I possibly have forgotten?" The man said, "There is no door knob. There is no knob on the door."

The artist smiled and said, "Oh, there is a door knob all right. Only, the door of life opens from within, not from without." The same is true of us. We open the door of awareness from within. The doors of our hearts and minds that lead to greater life open from within, outwards. We are the only ones who can open these doors.

Say to yourself:

There is only one door I am going to open today and that

is the door of my mind, my heart, the door of life itself. I am going to open the door that leads to life more abundant and reap the benefits of life.

Just as people store preserves, canned goods and the fruits of the summer for winter enjoyment, so can we look into the storehouse of our minds and see the wonders stored there for us to enjoy. There are magnificent designs for living. Explore the depths of your being and you will find many opportunities.

Within you is the glorious expression of Life itself, but you must open the door. The Ascended Consciousness is knocking always, but you must hear and you must open the door. Remember, you are your own thinker. You are your own doer. You are your own designer.

If your life needs redesigning, open the door to your consciousness and begin to allow change according to the magnificent inner design. Keep on keeping on and you will reach your goal. Many times you may feel like giving up and quitting. You may feel like running away or hiding. But just remember to open the door and practice the Truth.

There are many quitters in the world today, far more than there are winners, and yet every quitter is a potential winner and every winner won because he or she didn't quit. It is those who keep on keeping on with a deep and abiding faith in truth and in life who win.

Sometimes we fall into such a routine that the vitality goes out of our lives. We just go on and on in our habitual patterns. However life should be continually fresh and interesting, provoking us to newness, beckoning us on to the next adventure. We are not just dealing with any old ordinary power when we deal with the Infinite. We are dealing with a power which gives us freedom to be, freedom to know, freedom to find out what is inside of us. We are all born in freedom, but we erroneously place ourselves in bondage. We lean against the door of life with our tensions, fears and pressures of all kinds, and often never let the door open wide for us.

You need to know that your own thought denies you the privileges of life or reaps its advantages for you. Many people who are wealthy are absolutely miserable and many people who have little are happy. It is all in the consciousness. Money is a medium of exchange. It is not wealth itself.

You must be rich in consciousness, not necessarily in stocks and bonds, though there is nothing wrong with stocks and bonds. You must be rich in consciousness first. Realize that your material wealth is the result of a wealth of consciousness. Touch the law of abundance and feel the prospering power of Mind. Daily you must enrich your thought. You must move away from poverty in consciousness and from images of lack and loss.

Know that if you keep the door of life wide open the riches of the Infinite will bless you. Say to yourself each day, "I am supplied with a richness of ideas. I let these ideas work for me. I realize that the door of life opens from the inside out. I do not look at effects but turn to the cause of my good. I know it is Life's good pleasure to give me all riches and good things, but I must keep the channel clear. I must keep the door open."

We must not only keep the door of life open to receive our good, but also we must keep our good in circulation in order for it to increase. Our joy will increase, our health will increase, our strength will increase, and our opportunities will increase. Everything in our life will prosper and increase.

The first thing to know about prosperity is that your good does not come from the outside. It comes from within. The second thing to know is that it is the open hand that gives *and* receives. Anything you have that you do not use, you will eventually lose.

Say to yourself:

I am prosperous. I am prosperous in mind, heart, body and spirit. I am prosperous in health. I am prosperous in ideas. I am prosperous in love. I am prosperous in friendship. I see and feel the prospering power of the Infinite flowing through me. I receive my good, and I share my good. I keep my good in circulation and it is never ceasing.

If you do this, the doors of life will open and your demand will be met. The law of increase will bring your good into your life.

No Enemies

The universe is on your side. There is nothing in this whole universe that is against you. There is nothing in this whole universe that is out to get you, but just as the universe is not against you, neither does it play favorites. It is wholly impartial in its love and givingness.

When you have this grand idea of the universe, petty annoyances fall by the wayside. You can forget the little things that upset you. You know there is nothing in all of creation that is against you. Everything is for you.

Who, then, is holding what against whom? We are holding everything against ourselves. If there is nothing that is ever against us, it is *we* who have created the problems. It is we who are feeling that something is against us. But this is all healed when we are completely absorbed in the consciousness that Life is always for us.

It is fantastic, absolutely fantastic, to be in this state of consciousness. We move out into our world with a wonderful feeling of belonging. We begin to see evidences of caring and sharing that we were not aware of when our attention was focused on our hurts and disappointments. We realize that others care that we are alive.

It is important for us to know that the whole universe loves us and needs us, and to move in that awareness daily. In this consciousness peace is realized and there is no longer frustration and confusion. There is no longer duality and inner conflict.

If you get in a state of conflict and confusion until everything in you cries out, "I would give anything for peace of mind," remember that not the universe or anything in it are against you. Everything is for you. Be still and let peace take over again. Say to yourself:

This conflict can only mean that I have forgotten the universe is for me and that I am one with the universe and everything in it. I let go of this conflict, this turmoil, and get back into my natural harmonious state of oneness with Life. I let the peace that is within me quiet my mind, my heart and my emotions. I am back on center again.

The more we move toward a greater realization of oneness, the more we express creatively and powerfully. When we enter into a feeling of realization of our unity, something happens. We begin to experience a new state of consciousness. If a parent should look at a child and say, "She's my problem. There's my problem right there," that would be seeing separation. But if the parent can feel unified with the child, there is no problem.

Viewing any situation from this level of consciousness gives us an entirely new outlook.

There is no problem in Mind. I am not referring to the human mind. I am referring to Universal Mind. There is no problem in Universal Mind. When you can get back to the

Source and realize this, life becomes much easier.

The Science of Mind teaches some wonderful principles and can help anyone who will apply the teachings to achieve a healthier, happier and more productive life. The principles, however, cannot simply be read and agreed to. They must be taken to heart and acted upon. We cannot change these principles nor can we bend them one iota, but we can move with these principles and work with Law.

We can affirm, declare and read endlessly without the desired results. Healing, whether it be of body, mind or emotions, comes about only when we get back to the Source and experience our union with the whole of life. The greater our realization of unity, the more creativity is expressed through us.

If you are indulging in erroneous ideas about yourself, others or life in general...if you are suffering in any way...by changing your consciousness, you can erase the erroneous belief. If you put a problem in arithmetic on the blackboard and then work out a wrong answer, all you have to do is erase the incorrect answer and work the problem correctly. You can do the same with your incorrect thinking. You can repattern your thinking. You can reeducate your mind. You can retrain your emotions and you can reorganize your habits.

The easiest way to do this is to approach it from a central starting point. That is, get back into right relationship with Spirit and feel centered in it. When you start from this point in consciousness, it is amazing how all your other relationships change for the better. You first get a right idea about yourself and then about others.

I believe what we really want to know in life is the truth about ourselves. We may evade and do all kinds of things to procrastinate in our quest, but underneath all this is the desire to know who we are, what we are here for and where we are going. These are the eternal questions of humanity, and only each of us individually can answer them for ourselves.

Sometimes we become discouraged in our search for answers, perhaps because we have looked for them in the wrong places. We should remember that just as the questions are the longings of our own consciousness, so are the answers provided by our own consciousness.

Say to yourself:

There is nothing within me that denies my good. There is nothing within me that denies my prosperity. There is nothing within me that denies me the right job. There is nothing within me that denies me love and companionship. There is nothing within me but the wonderful realization of my oneness with Infinite Intelligence, the source of all supply of every kind and description.

What is inside of us is what counts, not what appears on the outside to be causing us unhappiness or problems. Because our nature seems to get us off the track now and then, we must constantly be aware that the universe is on our side. There is nothing in the whole universe against us. We are one with it.

Say:

I affirm my oneness with life today. Turning my attention away from problems, I keep in alignment with my Source, from which my every need is met.

Staying on Principle

If you have a true understanding of Life, there will be no fear in you because you will know that good exists in every situation. You may have times when you say, "I don't know which way to turn," but you will know that the end result will be favorable to

217

yourself and all others concerned.

As long as you recognize that there is one final Power, one ultimate Power for good, you will not stray too far from home base. Say to yourself in times of stress, "I know there is only one ultimate and perfect Power. That final Power is infinite. Its expression is good and the end results have to be good, though I may not be able to see this good every step of the way. I rest in confidence as to the right outcome."

Suppose you have just been laid off or received a cut in your salary. At the moment it is not easy to see your good. You might think, "After all I have done for that company! I have given it the best years of my life!" You are irritated and angry, and as long as you are, the outcome of this situation will not be good. Why? Because your thoughts and feelings are not conducive to a favorable outcome. You have assumed the identity of the victim. In the role of victim there is continued loss, more loss and the magnification of pain.

At such a time, you must work on yourself. This is easier said than done, for you are in no mood to practice the Truth. You are all stirred up. You are filled with self-righteous indignation. You feel you are in the right, so why should you have to work on yourself? Nevertheless, it is the only way out of your dilemma.

Practice these ideas daily, then they will be easier to apply in times of stress. It is as if a man tried to lift a 500-pound weight. If he began with a small weight and built up his muscles, he could eventually lift the entire 500 pounds. The same is true in learning to play the piano, to sing, to dance, to write or to paint. It takes practice, a lot of practice to achieve the desired end. Is there less reason to practice knowing the Truth?

Everything looks easy once a skill has been learned, but you can be sure that it was not easy in the beginning. It took a great deal of practice. Remember, you must stay right on base and when things go wrong you must recall that good is always present in every situation.

Here is an example which might help. When I first started to study Truth, I likened it to a fireplace. If I stayed close to the fire I felt its warmth and comfort, but if I moved away from it I would feel less and less heat. The fireplace would still be there roaring, but I had moved away from it. The fireplace did not move; the fire did not go out but I moved away. If we move mentally away from Truth, it cannot work for us the way it might.

We must eliminate every belief in our consciousness that has a tendency to divide us. Look into your consciousness and ask, "What is inside of me that divides me from the whole? What doubt? What belief? What image? What feeling? What is it within me that is keeping me from experiencing the unity of my being?"

When you eliminate all division, the moment you are aware of it, you will get right back into the unity of the whole. In doing this, you turn within yourself and say, "Here is a belief that divides and does not unify. Here is an image that divides and does not unify. Here is a negative statement I have been saying to myself that divides and does not unify." Many times we will find more in our consciousness that divides than unifies.

When that happens, we must get back on center, and to do this we must practice. We must constantly remember that there is nothing in the whole world that can hurt us if we remain centered in spiritual awareness. No one has the power to hurt us. So long as we know that there is nothing in the universe that is out to hurt us, we will cease to give power to others to do so, and we will cease to open the door of our consciousness to hurt.

Only you can know why you hurt. Only you can realize the damage which takes place when you let yourself be hurt. Ask yourself if you have hurting thoughts about other people, about your business, about a competitor, about a loved one. If you do, you are not experiencing the unity of your being. Be very honest with yourself. You cannot afford to hold any hurt toward any individual, because the hurt you hold toward any individual is hurt you ultimately hold toward yourself.

No one can infect your mind. No one can infect your consciousness. Any infection we have, we have given to ourselves. We infect ourselves with our own thoughts and feelings. We create what is in our own consciousness and then we experience what it brings forth. Maybe you don't hurt or bear grudges, but you fear, you doubt, or you feel unloved. Whatever it is in you that gets you off-center, face up to it and then turn again to the practice of Truth so you will be back in balance, back on center.

You will find if you stay in Truth that you can totally disagree with other individuals and still love them. You do not have to be a doormat. You can be yourself and let the other individuals have their own ideas and opinions. However, you will not be staying in truth if you harbor hurtful thoughts of any kind. When you do, it is like having a low-grade fever. You are not sick enough to stay in bed yet you don't feel well enough to do much else.

If you have a low-grade fever mentally or emotionally, then you are letting something infect you. Whatever it is can be healed with one prescription, and that is to get realigned with Spirit and to practice Truth. We cannot kid ourselves that our problems or hurts will go away of their own accord. We must purify our consciousness so healing can take place.

If you are filled with love, you will experience love; if you are peaceful within, you will experience peace without. It is a rewarding thing to know that the one cure for all ills is always at hand. It is available to each and every one of us. You can be sure that Spirit is as near as your thought, that only one ultimate outcome can exist in the universe and that it is good. Stay on center and experience your good.

Say:

Infinite good is mine today. I keep myself centered in Truth and the way is made clear before me. I practice Truth in my thinking, in my emotions, and in my actions. The outcome can only be good and more good.

Expecting Miracles

There is a Power that definitely heals, restores, transforms and makes whole. This Power works in your life every minute of every day. It does not take a vacation or a holiday. It is always working and always workable, but it can work much more effectively in your life if you work with it, if you believe in it, if you trust it.

You may have a problem and not consciously know the answer, but the answer is there. The problem is nothing more than a challenge to you to use your abilities and capabilities to a fuller extent. You call it a problem rather than a challenge because you are looking at the wrong side of the coin. Turn it over and see the answer. This is one means by which you grow and expand your consciousness.

You may not know what to do or how to do it, but the Spirit within you knows. Be still and listen. Say to yourself, "I release this difficulty. I release this trouble. As I release it, I turn in consciousness to the answer. I call upon Spirit within me to reveal the way to me."

You do not have to figure out the "how." Remember that the Power is always for you and always working with you. The moment you establish this consciousness, you will know that you are working from the very truth of your being. This knowledge will give you a sense of freedom, even if outwardly the problem has not already resolved itself.

If you have a problem, you are not weighed down; you are not caught; you are not trapped. You are free. You are already free of the difficulty you are experiencing. You are free of that which is unpleasant. You are free of that which is dragging you down. You are free. You are free to choose, to act, to grow. You are free to receive in consciousness the solution to what you are calling a problem. Get this sense of freedom, for the law of attraction will draw unto you that which you believe.

Say:

I am now accepting a wonderful new state of conscious-
ness. I am now accepting the solution that I know is
already present. I reposition myself in consciousness. I look
at the other side of the coin.

All things work together for good when you place yourself in the hands of Universal Life. Remember, what you decide about your life right now is what counts, not what you thought an hour ago. Give no thought to the morrow. Concentrate your thought on the present. All that matters is that you know your life is being transformed right at this moment.

Do not look for the change. Do not try to measure it. Accept it. Say:

My life is being renewed. My business is being healed. My
body is being transformed. Every situation in my life is
being changed for the better. There is a divine Intelligence
within me. I let go and let my good unfold.

Expect a miracle. Do not dig up the seed to see if it is growing. Know that it is, because its nature is to grow. If you look for the miracle or dig up the seed, you are not trusting implicitly in the Intelligence within you. Don't wonder, "Is it working?" Know it is working. Leave it alone and see the miracle happen. Let the miracle happen, knowing that a miracle is a natural happening in Spirit, but one that seemed impossible when you were depending only on your finite mind.

Today, let go of what is finished. Do not hang on a little longer. That will only delay your demonstration of good. That will only hold your miracles back. Do not try to feel one way and act another. You cannot say beautiful words about miracles and at the same time feel that nothing is going to happen. You must go all the way with both your thoughts and feelings, then when you get the inner signal to do so, you must act.

You cannot feel poor and expect to manifest abundance. You cannot say you love then act hatefully toward others and expect to experience love. You cannot say "I feel lousy" and expect to experience health. You must have the single eye, the single mind, for miracles to happen.

When you say "God is love," do you feel love? If you say "peace" and feel nothing but war within yourself, you must do something about it. If you say "Life is abundance" and then see nothing but poverty about you, something is wrong in your consciousness.

There is a divine design within you. That design is made up of joy, of health, of peace, of love and of prosperity. Look within yourself and find this design and then work along with the divine Architect in bringing it forth in your life. As you build a beautiful life according to this perfect design, miracles will begin to happen.

Everything that is good and beneficial to your life is obtainable. Your good is always within reach. The healing of any problem is always available to you. With your uplifted consciousness all things are possible. That which you try completely alone may be aborted along the way, but when what you do is in alignment with and in accord with Spirit, you can be sure of accomplishment.

The Spirit within us is always expanding. If we do not expand with it we begin to limit ourselves, and as we limit ourselves we experience pain in some area of our lives. There is only one Spirit and it is omniscient, omnipotent, omnipresent and omniactive. We live and move and have our being in this universal Power, Intelligence and Activity. If it is ever expanding and never stands still, we must also be constantly unfolding more of the potential that is within us.

One of the beauties of life is that it is constantly moving out into new areas of creativity. When we try to cling, hold on, stand still and not let go, we are bound to experience discomfort of some kind. We are bound to feel limited and restricted because we are not keeping up with the urge of Life to express within us.

From the moment of your birth, you started life in a new dimension. You have always had life and you will always have life, since you are infinite and eternal, but the life you are living on this earth is a new experience. There is a purpose for your being on this planet at this particular time and place. Part of this purpose is to receive; part of it is to give. Part of your purpose for being here is to grow and fulfill the requirements that lead to a larger, finer expression. You are constantly in progress. You are a process that is constantly taking place. While you are here, let the Life within you unfold in as many fulfilling ways as possible.

Since you are in a process, you are always becoming more of that which you are. You are always studying, always uncovering, always realizing more. This is the great beauty of Life. If you consciously move with the process, your life will unfold in harmony. You will be able to accomplish with grace and ease.

Things which were previously impossible to you will become possible.

This is why I can say to you that everything good and beneficial to your life is attainable. The healing of the body, the mind and the emotions is always at hand.

Whatever you think needs to be healed, work with spiritual principle and the healing will take place. When you work with univeral Intelligence, many beautiful and wonderful things become possible.

If your life seems chaotic, get back on center and everything will begin to flow in perfect law and order. The Creator fashioned everything in perfect harmony. The Creator is infinite intelligence and divine love. It is everywhere present. It is within you and works through all its creations. When you work with this Power and Presence within you, you have the power of the universe back of you. If you want to succeed, you must relate to this Great Whole. You must relate to that which is perfect. You must relate to that which is harmonious. You must relate to that which is ever-expanding. If you relate to that which is failing, to that which is dying, to that which is chaotic or to that which is negative, Universal Law works negatively for you.

Say to yourself:

I know my good is everpresent, for Infinite Intelligence is within me, working in perfect order through me. Nothing is impossible to me when I work with the infinite Source. My attitude is always one of gratitude, for when I move to accomplish, I know my need is already met.

Realize today that whatever is true about Life is true about you. Since this is so, your good is always at hand, always available to you. Whatever needs to be healed in your life or made possible is even now being done unto you—because of your belief.

Chapter Thirteen

~~~

Enlarge
Your Vision

The real voyage of discovery consists not in seeking new landscapes but in having new eyes.

—Marcel Proust

~~~

Where there is no vision, the people perish...

—Proverbs

~~~

For I dipt into the future, far as human eye could see, saw the vision of the world, and all the wonder that would be...

—Alfred, Lord Tennyson

Sometime ago, I read of a college student who was studying to become a scientist. He was excited about experimenting with all aspects of life, and on this particular occasion he was watching a butterfly struggling to free itself of its cocoon.

He thought, "Here is where I can step in and help." He took a very sharp instrument and slit the sides of the cocoon so it would open more quickly and the butterfly could emerge. The butterfly did emerge. It flew out of the cocoon—and fell to the ground. It started to fly again, and once more fell to the ground.

The student discovered that his plan to help the butterfly was actually a liability. During its struggle to free itself of the cocoon, the butterfly develops its wings. It gains strength in its struggles. It develops all it needs so when it does leave the cocoon, it is strong and complete and is able to operate on its own.

Many of us find ourselves as butterflies in a cocoon. It might be a cocoon of low self-esteem. It might be a cocoon of emotional distress. The cocoon is whatever seems to be imprisoning us, what seems confining and restrictive.

Life calls for strength. We need insight. We need courage. We need greater awareness, and often we want to attain these in an easy way. We do not want to struggle. We do not want to put forth any effort.

I don't believe life should be a fight and a struggle, but I do believe that when there are difficulties in our lives which have to be faced, we cannot always avoid them. We gain strength by facing up to what must be confronted. We grow through experiencing and overcoming.

In the case of the butterfly, someone intervened, someone was trying to help, but in his attempt he prevented the butterfly from gaining the strength it needed. We do the same thing to our children when we overprotect them, when we do not let them bear their own responsibilities or try their wings on their own.

It is not only our children whom we try to assist in ways that are not helpful at times, but our friends and relatives, too. Sometimes when a person is ill, we do not let him exercise sufficiently to gain more strength. I am not implying that we must fail to provide every attention and care that he needs, but doctors have learned that an individual regains his health more quickly if he is expected to do for himself what he can do.

Husbands and wives sometimes make their spouses dependent on them in areas where they should depend upon themselves. We allow friends to lean on us too much sometimes and then wonder why they do not gain strength of their own to carry on with their everyday problems.

How, in fact, do we develop our own confidence? How do we learn discipline? How do we develop character? Certainly not by standing by on the sidelines and letting someone else take over for us. The only way we can unfold and expand is through developing our mental, physical and emotional strengths.

We let appearances throw us. The student looked at the struggling butterfly and in sympathy reached out to help. We look at someone involved in extricating himself or herself from a cocoon of some kind, and we want to reach out and help. But in doing so, we should look beyond the appearance. We should determine how much help we can give that is real help and not a hindrance.

Suppose you are struggling to extricate yourself from a cocoon of some sort today. You do not like the feeling of struggle and strain. If I waved a wand and made everything all right, would you really be any better off? All I would have done in such an instance would be to give temporary relief of a sort. You would have gained nothing from the experience.

If we are in a cocoon, we are likely to say, "I am struggling in my business. I am struggling with my health. I am struggling financially. I am struggling in my marriage." Here the focus is only on the struggle. However, the consciousness of the butterfly in the cocoon is not that of struggling. It is only aware of its desire to fly, and it is taking the necessary steps to gain sufficient strength to do that.

The butterfly, when it gains strength to fly, is not going to squeeze itself back into that cocoon again. You say, "Of course not," but how often do we, even after we find a solution, go back to our problem again? How often do we still think about it and talk about it? We live with it. We just won't let it go.

As soon as we awaken in the morning, we stir up the problem and start thinking about it all over again. Remember, the butterfly does not have this consciousness. As soon as it leaves the cocoon, it leaves the cocoon consciousness behind. It thinks only of flying, of what is ahead. It does not look back or try to drag the cocoon around with it.

Today, know that you can only have freedom from a cocoon if you leave the cocoon and don't turn back once you have extricated yourself from it. You can only expand by leaving the lesser for the greater. You cannot expand as long as you insist on holding on to the lesser. You cannot expand by holding on to yesterday.

Say to yourself:

I am ready to expand. I am ready to move out of this cocoon. I am ready to leave the bondage behind. I will not try to return to it. I will not drag it around with me. I know that I gain strength by facing whatever I have to face. I know also that appearances can be deceiving and that they are not reality. I turn to the reality of my being for divine guidance. In helping others, I first let myself realize what is real help and what is interference. I have the vision for myself and others to look beyond the appearance to what is best for the future.

Once you have committed yourself to a larger life, move into it. Really let go of the consciousness that is finished. Remember that heaven means expansion. Move, then, into the Kingdom of Heaven and let the undefeatable Spirit within you take dominion over your life. Keep your vision high. It is only by losing your vision that you perish.

Chicken or Eagle

Often we forget what we are and who we are. We are spiritual entities with a dynamic mind, a dynamic spirit and a dynamic flow of life, but when we forget who we are, we do not express our true nature.

Emerson said, "To imitate is suicide." Of course it is. It is trying to be something we are not. It is keeping the real self from expressing.

We want to be accepted. We want to identify with others, but we should never do so at the expense of our own uniqueness. That is too great a price to pay. No two people are alike. There is something different about each one of us which makes us originals, and we cannot act or react just like someone else. We should be aware of this when we believe we may be following the crowd too closely.

Feel within you your spiritual consciousness. Raise your consciousness above the crowd. Dare to stand out in your uniqueness. Stand for what you believe in and express the intelligence and creative spirit that is within you. This is not to imply that you are somehow better than others. It is a mandate to be your true self in expression.

Look about you. Look at your surroundings and find the answers to these questions: Are you trapped in sameness? Do you believe that if everybody's got the flu you are going to catch it too? That if everybody is experiencing a recession you are going to experience it too? That if everybody is discontented you must be too?

Or is there something in you which says, "Rise, rise and look to that beautiful consciousness within you, the beautiful spirit that elevates you. Know the spirit of love, the spirit of intelligence, and the spirit of joy. It is all yours to realize."

It is my personal belief that each and every one us should see ourselves as a living, loving temple of Life. The Psalmist put it beautifully when he referred to abiding "under the shadow of the Almighty." When we do this, we know that we are never alone. We know that we can extract whatever we need from this great, infinite storehouse. We can do this through the power of

233

Spirit within us and at the same time never deny anyone else.

How can you take from someone else when the supply is infinite? You cannot as long as you "abide under the shadow of the Almighty," for you are drawing from unlimited substance, unlimited supply. How do you partake of this abundance?

You partake by aligning yourself with it in consciousness, by aligning with whatever you deeply desire. Like an eagle, then, take wing and fly. Do not look back. Do not be drawn back into the sameness that makes you an imitator instead of an initiator. Feel your absolute freedom. Remember, Life is affirmative in its nature and it is always pulsating with newness, not oldness.

The life within you is never bound nor restricted. The soul within you is never a prisoner. You are a free agent and you have a right to feel free. You do not need the armor of sameness to feel that you belong. This marvelous, creative intelligence within you enables you to know that you are a child of the universe. This life within you surges forth into creative expression and nothing can hold you back—and you belong, you always belong, for there is no separation between you and the Power, between you and others. There is just the same infinite Whole.

When you develop an eagle consciousness and know you can fly, you can do anything you desire to do, providing you keep your contact with Spirit. Forget this, and the wind is taken out of your sails and you drop earthward. You find yourself pecking among the chickens again. The dullness comes back; the sameness enters in. You begin to imitate.

Be determined to remain linked in consciousness with the Power that makes all things new. Continually remember that we, of ourselves, can do nothing, but that the creative Power within us can do all things. Our part is to know who we are and to act accordingly.

Today, let the spiritual giant within you come forth and

express. Let it be your meat, your drink and your life. Let everything else in your life be secondary. Link up with First Cause and feel the reality of life, the Power and the Presence that are within you. This Power is yours today, but you must recognize it. You must accept it. You must know yourself to be it.

Words are only sounds in the air or scratches on paper until we put them to work in consciousness. Do not, then, say, "All this sounds great, but will it work in my life?" It will work in your life, but you must accept it and allow it.

Say to yourself:

I am free. I am healed. I look forward and not back. I know who I am, where I am going and what I am going to do. I am guided and directed by the Spirit within me, which is surging forth into new and wonderful expression each day. I live a unique, original life, because Spirit creates me to express in a new and different way, not in the same way as anyone else.

Be thankful for this new state of consciousness and know that old habits have no power over you. The condition or situation which was bothering you no longer has any power over you. Put the old sameness consciousness behind you and move lovingly and bravely into the new life that is before you. Greet it with arms wide open, to receive the good it has to offer you.

Expand Your Vision

There is no true value in living until you feel you are in the process of becoming what you want to be. First, though, you must *know* what you want to be. You must feel deeply within you what you want to express in this life. Then you can say to yourself, "This is what I want to do. This is what I want to experience. This is what I want to express."

Your thoughts and feeling will be different from those of others. Even identical twins are separate individuals. They are not carbon copies of each other, though they may look alike. They have their own thoughts and their own dreams. Neither are you a carbon copy of anyone else.

What you really love to do, you will do well. Therefore, claim each day that there is an infinite Intelligence guiding you in every way to do what you will love to do. Speak to your subconscious mind and claim each day that universal wisdom is your wisdom and that you have access to that wisdom. There is a spark of divinity within you, but you must claim it. By claiming it, you activate it in your life and find who you truly are.

When I was going to college and a test came up, I learned not to be concerned about it, because I realized they were not trying to find out what I did not know but what I did know. I knew the Mind that asks the question is the same Mind that answers the question. I knew also that the answers were within me, for I was using the same Mind the professors were using. Of course I had to learn the material consciously, but this perspective nevertheless gave me a great sense of release and relaxation. No one was really testing me, because the answers were already in Mind.

Know today that there has to be an answer to every question, and since you are using the one Mind, that answer will be revealed to you. This does not mean you do not have to study. This does not mean that you do not have to prepare yourself. It does mean you are working in the one Mind and can throw fear out the window and begin to grow up in consciousness.

Life is not testing you. Life is giving you an opportunity to reveal what you already know. Every day you have an opportunity to express more of yourself. No one is trying to test you or catch you off base. Life does not test you or punish you.

The greatest discovery you can make for yourself is to know that you are part of this great inner Power and that it is directing you and revealing itself through you. When you realize this, you will open up whole new vistas of consciousness within yourself. Choose this day, then, what you want to experience in your life. Say to yourself, "Today I choose happiness. Today I choose health. Today I choose success. Today I choose right action. Today I choose peace." Choose, for the choice of your life must be yours. If you choose constructively, then you will always find yourself in a consciousness of expansion.

When I first entered into the study of Truth, I found myself on a mediocre level of life. When I realized I was on this level, I said, "All right. If I believe that I am part of an expanding consciousness, then my life should be constantly upgraded. There should be a constant improvement." There was great joy in seeing that my life did improve. I went from one apartment to another, from one car to another, from one level of living to another, from one neighborhood to another. These were only outer effects of an inner expansion, but they made me realize that I truly was a part of this ever-expanding universe of intelligent action.

You can expand your idea of health. You can expand your idea of art and talent. You can expand every gift you have. You can expand in every way, because you are part of a great expanding idea. You are part of an expanding world. The universe is infinite and it seeks to expand through the consciousness of every individual upon the face of the earth.

Say, then, to yourself:

Today I expand my idea of myself. Today I expand my concept of myself. Today I expand my belief in myself. What I believed yesterday belongs to yesterday. What is important is what I believe today.

You will never get old and you will never get stale and you will never know anything that won't give you joy if you become captivated by the wonderful consciousness of who and what you are. Know you are an expanding idea in Universal Intelligence. Know that the Infinite expands its creativity by means of you. Know that as you enlarge the container of your consciousness, day by day more of the riches of the universe will fill it.

Do not be concerned about "the good old days." It is today that is important. Today is now. Do not restrict and constrict your consciousness by dwelling on the past. The future has greater promise than you have ever dreamed of or realized before. Prepare your consciousness by expanding your vision. Ask yourself, "How much can I believe?" Then know that you can believe as much as you can accept, and give thanks for your good. Thankfulness is important. Thankfulness for your good even before it is apparent in form is evidence of your faith.

Each day sit down and image in your consciousness your fulfillment. Do this actively until you feel fulfilled. In the next breath do not say, "Now, let's see if anything happens." If you are spiritually fed, you *know* you are fed, just as you know you are no longer hungry after eating a satisfying meal. Say to yourself:

I expect to be joyously and spiritually fed. Consciously and
subconsciously I accept the fulfillment of my vision. I feel
it is the truth of my being now. I feel renewed. I let it go. I
now release it completely to Universal Law.

In Job 22:28, we read these words, "Thou shalt also decree a thing and it shall be established unto thee." Sometimes we feel that we ourselves are doing the creating in our lives, but in truth something greater than ourselves does the creating. We only provide the pattern. What this quotation is telling us is that within us we have the key to the kind of life we want to live. It is telling us that what we desire with all our hearts and minds will come to pass, if we believe it will. We need to picture and feel the fulfillment of our desire so that which we decree will be accomplished through us.

Job knew that what a man or a woman decrees will come to pass in his or her life. And it is important that *you* prove to yourself there is a response from an infinite Intelligence to your beliefs and your desires.

Any picture in your mind must have the substance of your conviction. If you are just letting pictures run through your mind to entertain yourself, you will not get results. That which you picture in your mind must be established with conviction. Fantasy will not do the job. Using the imagination as an escape will not do the job.

Know that you do not have to be a halfway person. You do not have to feel insecurity, old age, illness, or failure. You can constantly emerge from old concepts into new concepts of yourself and life. Begin to see yourself in the process of ever becoming more. Let each day be a new and rewarding experience for you.

Say:

I am a part of this great Power within me. Through me, it creates after the pattern I give it. I decree the desires of my heart, knowing they will be fulfilled.

Come to Life

As long as you think of yourself as just an average person, an average homemaker, an average husband and father, an average businessman or businesswoman, you will lead an average life. Why? Because you have trapped yourself in the ordinary. You see yourself as ordinary. You feel yourself as ordinary. You have forgotten how "fearfully and wonderfully" you are made. You have forgotten the creativity within you.

We live an uninteresting, mundane existence when we could be living vitally and creatively with a feeling of fulfillment and joy.

What we need to do, then, is to stimulate the life that is within us. We need to remind ourselves often how great we really are and how much more intensely life could be lived than most of us live it. Life, when we are alive to it in consciousness, is a very stimulating experience, and it should be.

One of the things which makes life stimulating is to lift yourself out of the ruts of old thinking and think new thoughts. One new thought will stimulate another. One new desire will impel you to move forward into new activities. You will begin to see yourself, others and the world in a different light. Nothing will any longer seem just everyday or average. Everything will take on a new fascination for you, because you will look beyond the external and see life seething and pulsating at the center.

You will be filled with new energy, new ideas. You will see things in a creative way. You will touch on new areas of consciousness. Life becomes magical, filled with wonder and delight. Others will benefit from this new, enthusiastic you, for when you are stimulated, you stimulate; when you are creative, you arouse the creativity in others; when you achieve a great success, others succeed too.

Say to yourself right now:

I am a creative individual. I stimulate my consciousness with possibilities of the new and the unusual. Nothing is ordinary. I see possibilities I have never seen before. As these possibilities grow and bear fruit, they benefit others as well as myself. Whatever I do is for the good of all concerned.

As an individual you are important. You are important because you are a unique expression of life. Only when you dare to be yourself do you fulfill yourself. The lima bean plant does not say, "I am more important than the tomato plant." The tomato plant does not say, "I am more important that the corn stalk." Each is willing to be itself without competing with the other.

Never think of yourself as competing with anyone other than yourself. Think of yourself as being the best you can be. Say, "I am only competing with myself. I love to compete with myself because I love to constantly outdo what I have done before." This is a healthy kind of competition. It keeps you from being too complacent.

Some authors write a book and it becomes a bestseller and they never write another bestseller. Other authors hit the market and have one bestseller right after another. Why? Because they are constantly outdoing themselves. The authors who have one bestseller and no others think, "I have arrived. I do not have to keep working." The other authors take the attitude that one bestseller does not mean they cannot exceed themselves and do better.

We cannot ride on the glory of past performances. That is living in the past. That makes us a "has-been." You become a has-been if all you can talk about is, "I remember when I had my bestseller. I remember when I scored my highest score. I remember this and I remember that...." When someone talks in this vein, I feel like asking, "But what have you done lately?" They have done nothing, because they are spending their time dwelling on what has been instead of what is present or ahead of them to do.

Now we do not have to amass huge fortunes, write one bestseller after another or cut a gold record every year. We do not have to do anything that the world calls great, but we do have to keep ourselves active and stimulated by constantly outdoing ourselves and not resting on our past achievements. We can never afford to become complacent and set. We can never allow ourselves to feel that we have achieved the ultimate.

All records are made to be broken. If you want to be a secretary, do not be content to be just an ordinary secretary. Strive to be the best. If you are going to be a plumber, do not be content to be an ordinary plumber. Be the best. Be the best that is in your power to be, not because you are competing with others, but because there is always more within you to be expressed. This is the way life thrusts itself forward through you. It never rests. It never stops. It never says "Look what I have done" and then rests upon its achievement. If it did, we would not exist for very long.

Look at birds, animals, plants, flowers, trees and people. Look at everything about you. What makes them interesting? The fact that they are growing and developing all the time. They are constantly moving from one stage of life to another. They are expressing and fulfilling the potentials within them. Life itself is so vast that you can never plumb its depths, but you can always draw from its depths new ideas for living and being.

Say to yourself:

Right within me is this unfathomable well of consciousness which contains all wisdom. I draw from it daily. It gives me the ability to succeed. It gives me the know-how to achieve. It gives me mastery over my life. It stimulates me to new growth and activity.

Begin right where you are to increase the expression of your life in every area. If you are awake, alert and alive in your consciousness, you will be amazed how your life will unfold. You will find that you have more courage, more faith, more ability, more of everything than you previously gave yourself credit for having. You will get a feeling of excitement and upliftment. You will realize, "I have only just begun. Come on, Life, let's go!"

Have you been standing offstage in the wings, or sitting in the audience simply looking on? Get on stage. Be the star of your own show. Of course, you have had setbacks and you may have some more, but they are not important as long as you get up and get at it again.

You have the stuff inside of you to be what you want to be. Do not let the evidence of your senses make you think to the contrary. They only record appearances. Do not let any external thing dull your sensitivity to the Power within you.

As I have said many times before, no one is born a loser. This includes you. You are tagged to win and it is impossible for you to fail if you team up with your inner assets. Do not quit, since life is always beginning anew for you, if you can but see it.

What is it you think you need in your life? What would you like to demonstrate? Does it appear dull and monotonous? Do you seem to be caught up in the trap of sameness? Don't turn your back on life. Face it. See what wonderful thing it has for you. When you team up with Spirit and let it stimulate you to live life vitally, you will know what it is like to be a real winner.

Say:

I let Spirit be my stimulus to new and fruitful activity. I realize I have only just begun. Come on, Life, I am with you!

Dare to Be Different

We can change our circumstances any time we decide to do so. To bring this about, though, will require a revolution in consciousness which breaks up the old and evolves into the new. It may not be easy at first, but it can be done. It comes, not by just thinking about it, but by giving birth to a new concept within the self.

One of the most pathetic types of individuals I have ever met is the kind who is forever apologizing. He goes through life constantly apologizing to others. No one has to apologize— often, it seems, merely for taking up space on this planet or for breathing the air and enjoying the sunshine. But no one needs to do that! After all, we are made of Perfect Stuff. Know this, and quit making excuses or apologizing for being alive. The Stuff that is in you is worthwhile, successful Stuff, because it is the Stuff of life. If one person fails and another wins, it is due to the way the proud, successful individual has used his consciousness. One makes an asset of it, another a liability.

Another pathetic type of individual is the one who goes to college and studies only those subjects that are most likely to result in making money. His talents may lie in a completely different direction. Later he will find himself dissatisfied, a square peg in a round hole. Remember, go with what you love to do and the way will open before you. The world needs all types of people and most of all it needs people who are happy and creative in what they are doing.

Do not go against the grain of your strongest desires and inclinations. Realize that whatever it takes to win, you have it within you. Don't conform just because it is the thing to do. Be yourself. I am not advocating rebellion, though. No. I am simply saying, "To thine own self be true, and it must follow, as the night the day, thou canst not then be false to any man." You owe this to yourself and you owe it to life, so follow the dictates of your heart.

Another area in which people tend to conform is in the area of clothes. Many feel they have to dress a certain way because it is in fashion. The fact that they look ludicrous does not matter—they are in style! To me the smart dresser is one who does not dress according to fashion, but according to what he or she looks the best in.

Just as everything we do reflects our way of thinking, so does the home we live in. If a house looks as if a cyclone has just struck it, then it is pretty certain that the person living there has a cluttered, mixed-up mind. It is all right to have a closet or a corner somewhere that catches the clutter, but when everything is out of place, that is a different story. An individual who never knows where anything is and can never find anything is living in confusion. That confusion is a waste of energy and time that could be put to use constructively.

Again, when I say, "Be a nonconformist," I am not saying, "Be a rebel against life." I am saying, "Be yourself." Everyone is different in some way. This difference is what makes you an individual, so be who you are!

You must find your own place in life. Then you must bring out your uniqueness through the creativity within you. You are different from any other individual on the face of the earth. If you dare to be yourself, you will be happy and prosperous and you will have something to give to the world. Say to yourself right now, "I am not going to be a conformist in ways that go against the grain of my being. I dare to be a nonconformist. I dare to be my own unique self."

We do not have to do everything that everyone else does and we do not have to look like everyone else looks. We do not have to think like everyone else thinks.

What you need to do, then, is to act out your true beliefs. You must express your true nature. Nothing will hasten you to your grave more quickly than trying to follow in the footsteps of somebody else. Nothing will give you more liveliness and vitality than to bring out the creativity within you in your own unique way.

Say to yourself right now:

I am a unique expression of the one Life. I have creative talents within me which are natural to me. In ordinary things I may conform, but when it comes to being myself and expressing myself, I am a nonconformist. I engage in activities of my own choosing in my own way. I accept the goodness and consciousness of my own being.

Look at the world. The doctrines and traditions of the world do not conform to one another. They are different. Neither do you have to conform to any doctrines and traditions. You can live in a new way. Each way is good for its time, but its time runs out and something new must take its place. Don't let yourself get trapped in old patterns and old ways. Wake up to your true self and live anew.

Say:

The dawn breaks new and fresh each day. The seasons change; new flowers bloom. New crops are ready to harvest. So is my life new each day. The creativity within me wells up in new expression to bless me and my world.

Chapter Fourteen

~~~

The Creative
Power of Love

Some day, after we have mastered the winds, the waves, the tides and gravity, we shall harness...the energies of love. Then, for the second time in the history of the world, man will have discovered fire.

—Teilhard de Chardin

~~~

Love is the self-givingness of the Spirit through the desire of Life to express Itself in terms of creation....Love is a cosmic force whose sweep is irresistible.

—Ernest Holmes

The mystery of life is revealed in the consciousness of love. Love is all-powerful. There is no condition in our lives that love cannot heal. There is no disease that love cannot heal. There is no emotional problem that love cannot heal. There is no financial lack that love cannot heal. There are no disrupted relationships that love cannot heal. Why? Because love is a creative, cohesive power.

The key to the mystery of life is love. We must learn to love ourselves. We must learn to love what we are doing. We must learn to love where we are. If we do, we will be carried to great heights in consciousness.

The love I am referring to is the love of the heart. It cannot be forced, manufactured or pretended. It is not sentimental. It is an outpouring of goodwill and reverence for all life. Therefore, it is not limited to those in our immediate family. It radiates out to the hearts of all people and all things.

Whatever difficulty we may find ourselves in right now, no matter how insurmountable it appears to be, if we can meet it with the marvelous feeling of love, we can rise above it and do whatever is necessary to handle it.

By doing this we take all the strength out of the difficulty and put it where it belongs—within ourselves. In the face of love, a difficulty cannot advance; it cannot grow. It can no longer govern, because we are not handling it with anger or fear. We are not handling it with a feeling of negation. We are recognizing that, in reality, there is no difficulty, because love envelops all.

"But," you might say, "my difficulty is big. It is not a small difficulty." Then have a big love. Get into the feeling that there is no difficulty so great that love cannot and will not heal.

Suppose someone you love is afflicted with something called "disease" and this disease is given a frightening name. Every standard healing method has been tried. Many doctors have been consulted. Many different medications have been used. You say, "Name it, we have tried them all."

All right, in your concern for your loved one you have tried everything—you think. Today, let's try another prescription. Let's try a prescription of love. We have heard that love will heal anything. So why not try love?

I can hear you say, "But I have tried love." Of course you have. But it was probably "concerned" love, perhaps, a sentimental love—which may not be what was really needed. Instead try this prescription:

Saturate your loved one with the beautiful feeling that Infinite Love is giving power, strength, renewal, and healing. Let this feeling of love saturate every pore of his being. Bathe him in it. See him drinking it in. See every atom of his being aglow with it. Feel that where the love of Spirit is actively at work, nothing contrary to it can exist.

You can readily see that this is not a "concerned" sentimental love. It is a love of life, a love of being, a love that each and everyone of us has within us. It *releases* concern. It lets go of tension. It has no name for any disease, because in it no disease can exist. This love is the very Presence within. It is the very Truth within.

All difficulties and diseases can be healed by love. If you have difficulty in the office, try love. If you have a difficult parent-child relationship, try love. If you have a health problem, try love. Try love when fear, anger or hate appear. Whatever you are confronted with, try love.

Do not play at loving; really do it. Get the feeling of it. Know you are working with a principle that always works. Who does the loving? You do. Where does it originate? From you. It is not something that you manufacture. It is something that you recognize, something you feel, something you experience. All the while it is within you waiting to come into expression. It is that which holds you together and keeps you from falling apart. It is the power that gives you life and strength and intelligence. A lack of love will cause your world to fall apart. An experience of love will put it back together again.

There is no difficulty that love will not conquer. There is no disease that love will not heal. Isn't it worth taking a chance on love, especially when nothing else seems to work?

Trying love is something we have to do for ourselves. We have to love the real self we are. This is very important. If we had a healthy love of self, many of our problems would be eliminated before they began. Learning to love the self and the self of others is our greatest achievement in life.

Begin to love until doing so becomes real and natural to you whether you love is for yourself, for another or for any situation or difficulty that arises.

Say:

I know love is the answer to every problem or discomfort

that exists or appears to exist. Therefore, I use love, not a sentimental, concerned love, but the love that stems from the center of my being and radiates out to make right my world and the world of those I love. I feel this love welling up within me. I see it penetrating and absorbing everything unlike itself. I can always depend upon this love, for it is a quality of Divine Mind. It is an ingredient of the universe. I breathe love in. I exhale love. I see love in every person and thing in my life. I recognize that harmony, peace and love are the very substance of my life and beingness.

You can use this affirmation for yourself. You can use it when helping another. It is inherently a part of your life. You have but to realize its meaning and let it flow into your own world. There is no difficulty that love will not conquer. There is no disease that love cannot heal.

The Presence and the Power of Love

Why is it that love seems to be something few people ever truly experience? I believe it is because they think they have to seek love, that they have to go out somewhere looking for it. But the only place you will find love is within yourself, for love is the very core of your being. You are fashioned out of love, the givingness of Life, and you live and move and have your being in this love. You cannot be robbed of it, divorced from it or lose it, because you are the very activity of love. When Jesus told us to love one another, he was saying, "Practice what you really are."

Perfect Love is within me and within you. We are all of the same essence. We all dwell in the same universality. However, we all individualize this universality at the level of our

Therefore, it is not that we lack love. What we lack is the conscious awareness of it.

You can never separate yourself from the inner Presence, which is Love. Whatever happens to you, whatever you do or don't do, whether you experience joy or sorrow, sickness or health, infinite Love is present with you at all times. So you do not have to look for Love; you have to *recognize* it.

The world loudly declares the value of love, but the world is not experiencing love. Love that is born of passion and desire is not love at all. If we truly love, we do not kill that which we love, but nourish it. Love is something which frees us. We do not possess and are not possessed. True love permits us to be ourselves and lets others be themselves. It enables us to feel a healthy acceptance of ourselves, of others and of life. It helps us to understand ourselves and others better. It frees us from an excessive sense of responsibility for others, yet gives us an awareness of oneness with all others.

"If I give all I possess to the poor," says Paul in Corinthians (New International Version), "and surrender my body to the flames, but have not love, I gain nothing." He continues to tell us some of the things love is...and is not. "Love is patient, love is kind. It does not envy, it does not boast, it is not proud. It is not rude, it is not self-seeking, it is not easily angered, it keeps no record of wrongs. Love does not delight in evil but rejoices with the truth. It always protects, always trusts, always hopes, always perseveres." Is this the kind of love we radiate into our world? Until it is, our laws, our charities, our sacrifices will avail little except to exhaust our time, substance and energies.

Say to yourself:

I no longer seek after love. I no longer try to love. I know that Universal Love is within me is the core of my being. I do not create it, manufacture it, force it or find it. The

253

only thing I can do is to realize that love is what I am and what divine Mind is, what others are and what the world is. I let myself be love in expression today, for this is the natural expression of my being.

Today, distinguish between the desire that often masquerades as love and the Living Love, and you will begin to dwell in the consciousness of true love. You will find that this love heals and blesses and enriches. It always adds to and never takes from. In Spirit, which is Love itself, you will consciously live and move and have your being, and no outer turmoil can harm or disturb you.

The Waterbug Story

When we experience love, it melts away all that appears to obstruct. It creates a way for us to experience a greater expression of life. It gives depth and meaning. It puts joy and rhythm into living. Without love we seem to stand still and mark time. We feel heavy and weighed down. With love, there seems to be a constant surging or pushing up that takes us to new heights of awareness, to new realms of attainment. With love, we are not afraid to expose ourselves to all forms of love. Few of us realize that, at times, our only problem is that we have ceased to experience love and share this feeling of goodwill with others. We ride the surface of things. We forget to look beneath the surface.

It is not always easy to love the personality we know ourselves to be, but when we look inside and see the beauty of our true selves, it becomes easy. We are filled with amazement and wonder at what we really are. And we cannot know how wonderful we are without seeing how wonderful others are also.

That makes us eager to release this hidden splendor for all the world to enjoy.

Take time out to really look at yourself. Take time to glimpse the beauty which lies at the depth of your innermost being. Within you are greater treasures than all the silver, gold and jewels in the world.

To know yourself is to acquire wings in consciousness. You need respite from the business of the world, the hustle and bustle, the hurry and the confusion. You need to get quiet occasionally and say to yourself, "I am really going to take this time right now to know myself better. What is it that I need to know? What can I find within myself that will better acquaint me with myself?" Then turn within, stilling all outer thought, and listen. Gradually you will get beyond all obstructions and begin to see that which lies within your consciousness. You may have to do this many times before you become still enough and go deep enough for the answers to come. If you persist, however, the answers will come, and the experience is more than worth the time spent.

You can do the same with others. When you look at them, really look at them. Look into their eyes. These people are not what they appear to be. They are not what they act like. Don't judge them by appearances. Jesus, the teacher, told us not to judge by appearances. We are all much more than we appear to be. We are capable of being more, of giving more. That capacity is within every one of us.

The waterbug is a good example. It lives in water and mud and is about an inch and a half long, dark in color and clumsy in every way. There is nothing pretty about it. But you are not seeing the whole picture. At a certain point in the bug's development, it leaves the mud and the water and attaches itself to a rock. There, in the air and sunlight, this little bug with all the mud clinging to it begins to dry. As it dries, it even gets uglier than it was before. Naturally, in the sunlight, it begins to crack. It seems to split. As it splits, you begin to see some wings and then a goldish-green form emerges from the little circle of mud. The wings are gold and green and there before you is a beautiful dragonfly. It is the most beautiful of all flies. And yet, where was its beginning?

So you might look at yourself and your life and, judging by appearances, say, "My life is terrible. My life is unhappy. My life is barren. It is lonely." You may see nothing but ugliness, but you are looking only at the cover. Underneath is the beauty you are capable of expressing, just as the little waterbug was capable of becoming a beautiful dragonfly.

The waterbug had to leave its old surroundings and attach itself to a rock before it could express the beauty within it and take wing. Likewise you have to take your attention from the ugliness you may be seeing around you and attach yourself to a new state of consciousness. In this new state of consciousness you will find the beauty and the love that are within you and come into a new birth of livingness.

Say to yourself right now:

I turn away from the past. Whatever has been ugly in my life, I turn away from it. I leave the mud-consciousness of criticism, negation, self-condemnation and hostility. I fasten myself to the rock of principle within me. I see the beauty and worth of my true being. This enables me to love myself and to love others.

Stay with the idea that you are through with the mud, completely finished with it. Expose yourself to your true self until you emerge into a new state of consciousness and a new life.

No matter how ugly and unpleasant life appears to be, you

can take wing and be lovely, dynamic and stronger than you have ever been before. Feel the consciousness of love and life within yourself. When you do, you will live with a new consciousness, a new insight, a new aliveness.

Chapter Fifteen

~~~

Moving to a Higher Dimension

All are but parts of one stupendous whole,
Whose body nature is, and God the soul...

—Alexander Pope

~~~

Thou are thyself a fragment torn from God. Thou hast a portion
of Him within thyself.

—Epictetus

~~~

Whatsoever that be within us that feels, thinks, desires, and
animates, is something celestial, divine, and consequently imper-
ishable.

—Aristotle

*L*ife itself never causes anyone to enter into or remain in bondage. Life liberates us and gives us freedom in our livingness. Life, of itself, can never be bottled up. It is always expanding. It is never restricting or restricted.

You are always in the mainstream of life. You are an inlet and an outlet through which life flows. If you can accept today that there is no withholding on the part of life, then you have to recognize that you are the only one who can prevent your good from increasing. This "preventing" process, when it occurs, takes place in your mind. When you remove the blocks from your mind, the flow from the Infinite begins once more to occur.

However, it takes more to start this flow than just thinking positively. I do not believe we can accomplish anything in the world we want by merely thinking positively. We must go beyond just the mental and touch the divine Presence within us, which is the magnificent spirit and creativity of life itself.

This step is necessary because you are more than just

mental, more than just thought. You are more than a divine idea. You are the essence of love. You are the spirit and creativity of life. You are more than form and more than thought and more than feeling. You are an individualized expression of Infinite Being. You are life itself in all its potential.

Some people go through life and are aware of this indwelling presence, this aliveness within themselves. Others, not aware of it, look for it everywhere. But they who search for it will not find this Presence in a place like Mount Shasta or Lourdes. They will not find it in a tabernacle or a church...or anywhere else. It is not that this Presence does not pervade everything. It does. But when they find it, they will find it within themselves. That is where they must become aware of it. Once they find it within themselves, they will see it everywhere—including in all the places they searched and failed to find it.

And the eternal search goes on. We search in every book. We search in every nook and cranny of the globe. We look for a teacher who can show it to us. We search everywhere except the right place. We climb the highest mountain, search the darkest cave, and explore the deepest ocean to find our spark of divinity, and it is only when we have searched everywhere else that we turn within and find it where it has always been.

As long as we search the outer places of Life, we will be unsatisfied. When we begin to explore inner space, we will know that our search is at an end. Then, the beautiful experience begins, for as we turn to the Presence within, it turns to us. As we enlarge our consciousness, life expands its expression by means of us.

Already, here and now, you are a part of divinity. Realize this and look within. If you think you have experienced a great deal of hell in this life, know that you can just as well experience heaven. Both stem from within yourself, but until you know this truth, you will go on experiencing an up-and-down existence.

Infinite Intelligence does not find fault with you; you find fault with yourself. The spark of divinity is within you; you walk with it, talk with it and live with it. Your consciousness of it activates it within you. You dwell in it and it dwells in you. You do not just talk about it. You make contact with it. You let it have its way in your life.

"The world is so much with us" that we need to move deeper and deeper inside ourselves to really find the essence of divine life.

Inside of yourself you carry your own thoughts. You carry your own happiness. You carry your own unhappiness. You carry your own ill feeling and you carry your own opinions.

Therefore it is up to you to develop, deep within your own consciousness, the beauty and the rhapsody of that which is within you. You have heard people say, "Keep a good thought. Hold a good thought." We do not have to "hold" a good thought. We have to know the Truth. I do not believe that all the positive thinking in the world will truly heal anything. What we do must go deeper than that.

Inside of you is Life. Inside of you is Mind. Inside of you is the infinite Knower. Inside of you is that which is never depressed. Inside of you is that which knows absolute joy. You might say, "Well, where is it? All I know is misery, unhappiness and heartache. All I know is one problem after another. Where is this wonderful something you are talking about?"

Again, I say, it is inside of you and if you are not experiencing it you are not entertaining the kinds of thoughts that will permit it to shine through. You are not working with the right ideas.

Say to yourself:
I cease searching here and there. I turn and search within

myself. I touch the pure idea within myself and become aware of the Truth. This is where I find perfect Life. This is where I find illumination. This is where I find that spark of divinity which makes me one with the spirit of perfection. I search no longer in outer space. Inner space reveals to me all the wonders of the universe.

Remember that life never put you in a prison and if you are in one, it will never keep you there. Life flows in perfect freedom, expanding and increasing all along the way. It cannot suppress its creativity and its aliveness. If you are not experiencing it in its fullness, it is because you have let thoughts and things take precedence over Spirit. Once you turn again to the Spirit within you, your world will right itself.

Come down from the mountaintop, come out of the cave, and look in the only place where you will find what you are seeking—within yourself.

Say:

I touch Spirit within me and know my true wholeness. No longer do I search afar. I look within and accept what I truly am.

Today Is the Right Time

The real self is always invisible. The real you is within the form, but you are much more than that form, that body. You are Life. The thinker inside of you cannot die. You are immortal and the life you are is incapable of dying.

The real you is infinite. The real you is birthless, deathless, changeless and eternal. You do not suddenly become immortal. You are immortal always.

Expand your thinking. Expand your consciousness and

know that you always were and you always will be, that you never had a beginning and will never have an end. Your personality had a beginning and it will have an ending on this plane of existence, but not the real you. You simply express for a time as Mary or John or Suzie, then you go on to greater expressions.

Doesn't that stretch your consciousness? Doesn't that take you out of the little circle? Doesn't that take you out of pettiness, little thinking, and smallness of all kinds? You are universal consciousness. You can look at the sun and say, "I am that." You can look at the moon and say, "I am that." You can look at the ocean and the mountains and say, "I am that." You are everything. There is a part of you that is in everything.

I would like you to get this feeling that you are infinite. There is no limit to you, except the limits you impose upon yourself. It is done unto you as you believe, so give up the belief that you are mortal and subject to sickness, old age and death. Your soul is eternal. In dimensions other than this you will go on, constantly expanding. There are dimensions upon dimensions. I believe we have lived before and I believe we are experiencing a part of the Infinite right now. We come to a point of focus or expression here; we come to a point of focus or expression somewhere else. Maybe, in truth, we do this simultaneously, but the personality is only aware of it here at this time, for this is where our conscious focus is.

In a sense, we are all prodigal sons and daughters. We have wandered from the Source. We have moved away from the center, but there is always something within us impelling us back toward Spirit. When this urge is heeded, we move into a whole new consciousness.

Realize today: "There is no little me. I am infinite. I am filled with life. I am filled with vitality. I am filled with love. The joy of the spirit is upon me." This realization will get each of us out of the limited, restricted, negative concepts we have allowed ourselves to slip into.

We do not have to leave this life to start a new phase of living. We can do it any time we change our consciousness. Whether we are here or in another dimension, we will express at the level of our consciousness, for we attract to us what is in our thought.

It is always the right time to realize our oneness with life. It is always the right time to wake up to our potential. It is always the right time to change false beliefs. It is always the right time to look at and change the state of our consciousness.

Breakthrough to Newness

Life is a divine offering. It offers you challenges. It offers you opportunities. All is for your growth, and you can grow from every experience that comes your way, even the unpleasant ones. You grow through exposure to living. It is not that life is testing you or that you have to experience everything through the school of hard knocks. It is simply that there are many facets of reality and they are to us as we believe them to be. For example, public speaking is a delight to some people and an agony to others. It is a matter of your own individual frame of reference whether you consider something good or bad, desirable or undesirable, hard or easy. If it seems difficult to you, it may represent an area in which you need to grow and, therefore, to which you need to give more attention.

When you are driving your car up a hill, do you release the accelerator, or add more pressure to it? Certainly you add more pressure to it. You give your automobile what it needs to make the climb. Many of us, however, when we see a mental hill in front of us, or an emotional or physical hill, withdraw instead of accelerating.

When anything new or different confronts you, that is the time to accelerate your faith in Life. Just as you need to give your automobile more power to climb the hill, so do you need to release more inner power to reach greater heights of awareness. This is actually what growth is, an expanding of awareness from the known into the new and unknown. You cannot enlarge your consciousness by withdrawing.

Today if you are in a place or situation or frame of mind that is not to your liking, know that you are in the place where your consciousness has taken you. You are, then, in your *right* place, but this right place may not be the *true* place for you. There is a difference. We are always where our consciousness has brought us, but that is not always our true place, the place it is possible for us to attain.

Yet the more we feel we are in the right place, at the right time, doing the right thing, the nearer this comes to being our true place, since we are constantly repositioning and reorienting ourselves through experience. Further, the more we believe we are founded on divine love, the more we will trust this love to sustain and maintain us, whatever our outer experience.

Love is a healing power, a power for good. Let that power move through you. Let it bring new dimensions of awareness, even though the growth involved may at times be painful. The pain usually comes when we think we want to grow, but we also want to hold on to what we have. We do not want to change. It is like saying, "Yes, I want to grow, but don't disturb this; don't disturb that. Don't shove my life in that direction; don't move this." So our resistance to and, at the same time, our desire for growth causes pain.

Even a weed has to break the shell of its seed and then the

crust of the ground to be born anew. This is true of every plant, tree and bulb that grows. The old has to be disturbed for the new to come forth. A breakthrough requires a releasing for the new to come forth. A breakthrough requires a releasing of what was for the next that is to be. Without this releasing the new would not be possible.

We would grow with much less pain if we realized that all change is good, that it is going to bring something new and different into our lives. It is going to make us aware of new heights of beingness. When pain is involved in growing, that pain is minimized if we are not afraid of it, if we can see it for what it is—a breakthrough to new creativity.

Some people feel that they are on a merry-go-round and that it keeps going faster and faster. Their hope is that someday, by chance, they may get the golden ring and win a prize. If they are depending upon chance, then they are deluded, for there is no such thing as chance and there is no such thing as luck. The sooner they realize this and take their lives into their own hands, the quicker they will be off the merry-go-round and on a highway of adventure and discovery.

In taking your life into your own hands, do not pattern it after that of any other person. Draw upon the spiritual material within you and not the patterns of others. On every plane of awareness there is always the possibility of being new and original. Mind delights in expressing originality through its creation. Therefore, come into your own unique awareness today. Use the gifts that are within you. We have all been given the gifts of the Spirit. Some of us will use them one way and some another, but we all have the power to draw upon them to fulfill our own potential.

Greatness does not really involve doing some big thing. It involves fulfilling your own being in a greater way. Dare to trust and dare to believe that there is something in you and something all around you that you can rely upon. Know that this something is Infinite Spirit expressing by means of you. Give yourself willingly to growth and expansion.

Do not magnify pain, hardships, sorrow, hurts and disappointments. Take them in your stride. Go on through them. Say to yourself, "None of these things move me. I move through them to a greater awareness of myself and life." Do not let your spirit be dampened by adversity. Learn to turn adversity into victory in one way or another. This can be done if we are in the right consciousness.

If you choose to think of life as being drab and hard, you will develop a drab personality. You will look and feel old before your time. A dull and drab consciousness will attract everything of a like nature to it. The whole world will look gray to you and you will not see the beautiful or experience the good.

Say to yourself:

I choose to see the beauty of life. I allow this beauty to occupy my consciousness. Life is a wonderful opportunity for growth. I do not look for disagreeable people, for chaos and turmoil. I do not wallow in a pool of self-pity. I do not magnify pain or disappointment. I learn from them and move into a greater expression of growth.

Beginning today, instead of shying away from what seems difficult and hard for you, do that particular thing first. See what rewards it has for you. Live your life creatively with love and love will open many doors and make many pathways easier to trod. It will work miracles in your life as you grow and expand.

On Being Yourself

No two people experience life exactly alike. Each individual is a unique, divine idea of the Infinite. Everyone is also at a different stage of unfoldment in consciousness. Some develop more along one line than another. Therefore, each individual's world is different from that of others, yet there is always the underlying unity with the Whole.

These differences need not be in opposition. They can be complementary. That is why it is not necessary to insist that everyone conform to our own ideas and ways of life. The Infinite likes to express its harmony in multitudinous and original ways. This expression gives variety to the creativity of the universe.

We often try to figure out the ideal way that things should be and try to fit everything into the molds we have created. But life cannot be held in bondage to our concepts and creeds. It must expand. It must grow. It must express in new and different ways.

Say:

*I am spiritually centered and my life unfolds in wonder-
ful, unique and creative ways. I know and embody the
oneness and the perfection of life.*

We are basically spiritual, creative individuals. We are happy or unhappy depending upon the way we identify with life. We stifle the creativity within us if we try to feel and think and do exactly as others do. We should not try to fit ourselves into patterns that are not right for us.

The most important thing we can do is to know as much about life as possible and then use the creativity within us in ways which are original to us. We can identify ourselves as being a success or a failure. We can identify ourselves as being weak or strong. We can identify ourselves as being confused or harmonious. None of these identifications affects life itself, but they do affect *our* life.

We cannot change life itself. It goes on being creative. It goes on expanding. It goes right on being itself. We do, however, change our individual experience when we recognize that life is eternal and that it operates in accordance with Universal Law, which is awaiting our use. This awareness makes it possible for us to change our lives. It helps us to see that we are not trapped by circumstances and situations. It helps us to see the vital, living creative stuff of the universe that is ours to use, in any way we choose, for good or ill.

Life can always be depended upon. It is eternal. It is the basis upon which our very life rests, the wellspring from which it flows. Though it is always expressing more of itself, it has qualities which never change and in them lies our only real security. There is harmony, there is peace, there is wholeness, there is order, and there is love. These never change. They can always be depended upon just as can Universal Law which always acts according to its nature. It will not be erratic one day and stable the next. It can be depended upon.

We can be as original and as different as we choose. We do not have to conform. We do not have to squeeze ourselves into molds that constrict us. We can live vital, productive, happy lives in our own way as long as we maintain contact with the Source within us.

By Your Own Bootstraps

No condition or situation in the world can conquer the dynamic Spirit within us. Only when we give power to that which has no power do we feel helpless and hopeless. This undaunted, dynamic, undefeated Spirit is always there at the center, ready to radiate out and illumine our lives. When we are awake to Spirit and live from the center out, we flow instead of struggle, for we are moving in accord with the true nature of our being.

Yes, we can touch the external world and it seems real, very real to us. We cannot in the same sense touch the internal, unconditioned energy within us. That is, we cannot do so with the physical senses. But we can touch Spirit and feel our oneness with it by using our inner senses.

We are alive with a Mind that is formless. It is formless and unconditioned. It takes form by means of us and there is nothing we cannot do or be once we link ourselves with its power. Now, Mind may seem very abstract because it is invisible and because we cannot see, feel or touch it with our usual, everyday physical senses, but the physical senses are only small pinholes of awareness compared to the possibilities for awareness that lie within us. The purpose of our senses is to alert us to the physical world, the world of appearances. We must use our inner senses to know Mind and to expand our awareness.

Remember always to honor yourself as an individualization of the one Mind and not to compare yourself to another person. If you measure yourself against this and that, you will be batted back and forth like a tennis ball. If you take counsel with your fears and doubts, if you look only at your liabilities, you will surely convince yourself that you are a loser and can never make it. Take thought with whom you counsel.

Even though all appearances seem to be stacked against you, remember that oneness in consciousness with Spirit is a majority. Because the world of appearances is presented to us so strongly, we cannot always easily let go and turn away from it, but we must do so in order to find the power we need to manifest ever-increasing good in our lives.

Many of us feel the surge of Spirit and are carried along with it until fear knocks at the door, then we take our attention from Spirit and ask, "Who is it?" It says, "I am fear." Often we open the door and let it in. It is as if we say, "Oh, yes, fear, come on in." If, however, we are alert and aware, we will not answer the knock. We will say, "I remain constant in Spirit. I will not weaken."

Say to yourself:

There is no habit or condition that can turn me away from
Spirit. I am anchored in the spiritual integrity of my being.

Sometimes we are anchored only in our thoughts. We have to learn to walk away from our thoughts when they interfere with our lives. That means letting go of those thoughts which are hampering our experience. It means awakening from our negativity. It means awakening from our doubts and fears.

We can never overcome anything until we are willing to pick up our consciousness, pick up our thoughts, pick up our feelings, pick up our ideals, pick up our vision. But we cannot do that as long as we have decided: "This is my bed and I have to lie in it. This is my cross and I have to bear it. I know Spirit wants me to have this problem. I know Spirit wants me to suffer because of what I was in a former life, or because of what I did yesterday or last year."

Nothing is further from the truth. Spirit imposes no condition, situation or form of suffering upon us. There are those people who choose and enjoy suffering, but we do not have to be among them.

When we come to the realization that life is a joyous experience, we will find, if we have the right attitude toward it, that life can be a deeply rewarding adventure. If we will take the principles of the Science of Mind and apply them to everything —to our bodies, to our minds, to our emotions, to our finances, to our homes—these principles will work for us.

The kingdom of heaven, of expanded awareness, is within you. The kingdom of freedom is within you. Life is ever-unfolding and ever-growing, but we hold ourselves prisoners to our own thoughts, fears, habits and weaknesses. As long as we are our own jailers, we can not experience freedom.

Say to yourself:

I no longer imprison myself. I look within to the creative life that is mine. I know creative Intelligence keeps the whole universe operating in harmony and in perfect law and order. I recognize that creative Intelligence knows what to do, how to do it and when to do it. I feel my oneness with the Power, which is the only power there is. There is no other. I therefore give no power to things and situations. I unify with Spirit and my life operates as the universe does, in perfect law and order.

You are a spiritual entity. You are one with life. Remember who you are and identify only with the best of life—for that is what you are.

From Glory to Glory

The search is over. At last you have come to yourself. You and I have moved through your identity crisis together. We now agree that you are more than just a mere mortal. You are not a mere anything! You are the centralization of the divine Light, the divine Love, perfect Wisdom and creative Intelligence, focused in you, as you. Thus, understanding yourself, you pursue the highest creative art: the art of being yourself.

Being yourself is being in finite form what the Infinite is: Love and Joy having a creative adventure! How glorious you are!

How rich and rewarding the pursuit!

The next time a question seizes your mind, the next time you pause at the crossroads of a new beginning, remember that your ultimate guidance is within you, awaiting your call. Call forth infinite wisdom, divine guidance, knowledge, right action, and a heart stout enough to persevere.

Never have you been in a more advantageous position to express yourself and to succeed. The world is more receptive to creativity and originality than ever before. Innovation, both inner and outer, is literally to be the salvation of society. Use the creative mind within you to bring about a' more satisfying and harmonious lifestyle. Create a new approach to the "have to's" you tackle. Come alive at the workplace. Enliven your experiences at home...with your family...with your friends. Be healthier. Feel better. Be happier.

Isn't it wonderful that, having found yourself, you realize you were never lost? You can never be lost in a universe where there are no corners and all is known in Universal Mind. You will never be alone or unaided. Infinite Presence supports its own. The means for your support were inherent in your design. Complete and perfect, your mind has receptors and transmitters of which you are now aware. Simply attune yourself to the higher Intelligence and listen to the inner voice of divine guidance. It is always good. You are good. Now, let the good life unfold.